TExES

English as Second Language154

Practice Test Kit

Sharon A. Wynne

XAMonline, Inc.

Boston, MA

To obtain permission(s) to use the material from this work for any purpose including workshops or seminars, please submit a written request to:

XAMonline, Inc.
21 Orient Avenue
Melrose, MA 02176
Toll Free 1-800-509-4128
Email: info@xamonline.com
Web: www.xamonline.com
Fax: 1-617-583-5552

Library of Congress Cataloging-in-Publication Data

Wynne, Sharon A.

TExES English as a Second Language Practice Test Kit Teacher Certification / Sharon A. Wynne. ISBN 978-1-60787-389-1
1. English as a Second Language (ESL)   2. Practice Test.
3. TExES   4. Teachers' Certification & Licensure   5. Careers

Disclaimer:

The opinions expressed in this publication are solely those of XAMonline and were created independently from the National Education Association, Educational Testing Service, and any State Department of Education, National Evaluation Systems or other testing affiliates.

Between the time of publication and printing, state-specific standards as well as testing formats and website information may produce change that is not included in part or in whole within this product. Sample test questions are developed by XAMonline and reflect similar content to real tests; however, they are not former tests. XAMonline assembles content that aligns with state standards but makes no claims nor guarantees teacher candidates a passing score. Numerical scores are determined by testing companies such as NES or ETS and then are compared with individual state standards. A passing score varies from state to state.

Printed in the United States of America

TExES English as a Second Language (ESL) Practice Test Kit
ISBN: 978-1-60787-389-1

TABLE OF CONTENTS

1. **Language learners seem to acquire language by which process?** *(Average) (Skill 1.1)*

    A. A different process from learning in general

    B. A slower process than how they acquire their native tongue

    C. A gradual, hierarchical, and cumulative process

    D. A random process

2. **Mr. White's fourth grade ELLs are working in groups with native English-language speakers. The purpose of the activity is to have students: (1) identify root words and their meanings, and (2) see how prefixes alter the meanings of root words. Which of the following best describes Mr. White's thought in using this activity?** *(Rigorous) (Skill 1.1)*

    A. Knows the functions and registers of language and uses this knowledge to develop and modify instruction for ELLs

    B. Understands how listening, speaking, reading, and writing develops the ELL's English language proficiency

    C. Knows the benefits of having students work in groups

    D. Understands the importance of students learning the basic concepts of the English language

DIRECTIONS: Use the information below to answer the questions that follow.

In her fourth grade ESL class, Ms. Nelson had her students answer a prompt that required them to write three. The following is a paragraph written by Ishmael, one of her ELLs:

When Billy go two the store, he red a add for a sail on hot dogs. He buy 2. And eight them right then. He new he would be in trouble if his ant finds out. Becuz she is making a specail dinner. Billy leaves. He walked home.

3. **Based on Ishmael's writing sample, Ms. Nelson knew that she had to reteach which of the following English conventions?** *(Average) (Skill 1.1)*

    A. Homophones

    B. Phonographemic differences

    C. Homonyms

    D. Homographs

4. **Ms. Nelson plans to reteach homophones to her class, targeting the use of visual aids, such as illustrations, to show differences between homophones as well as using the words in sentences during discussions. Based on Ms. Nelson's plans, it is obvious that she is using which of the following adaptations?**
(Average) (Skill 3.2)

A. Nonverbal

B. Contextual

C. Paraverbal

D. Discourse

5. **Ms. Nelson also decides that, based on Ishmael's writing, there needs to be further work on which of the following?**
(Easy) (Skill 1.3)

A. Complex sentence structure

B. Use of compound sentences

C. Creating a simple sentence

D. Use of a compound predicate

6. **Changes in register are a result of which of the following sociolinguistic factors?**
(Rigorous) (Skill 1.2)

A. The person to whom one is speaking

B. Knowledge of the topic

C. Attitude toward the listeners

D. All of the above

DIRECTIONS: Use the information below to answer the questions that follow.

Mr. Sheffield wants to focus on developing students' speaking skills, so he engages his students in a discussion with his ESL class as to how their spring break was. During the discussion, all the students were comfortable participating and listening to each other. A portion of the discussion is shown below.

Mr. S: *I'm so pleased that so many of you had such a great spring break! Maria, what did you do over spring break?*

Maria: *My abuelita, my grandmother, came to visit. We had fun.*

Mr. S: *That sounds wonderful! I am sure you were happy to see her. David, what about you? How was your spring break?*

David: *I was sick most of the time.*

Mr. S: *I am so sorry that you were under the weather! That is not a good way to spend your vacation.*

At Mr. Sheffield's response, David looked confused and stopped participating in the discussion. While Mr. Sheffield noticed David's withdrawal, he continued the discussion before beginning the lesson. At the end of the class period, Mr. Sheffield took a few moments to speak with David and, at that point, David explained that he did not know what Mr. Sheffield meant by saying that David was *under the weather.* Mr. Sheffield realized his mistake, corrected it, and began to plan a strategy that would prevent this from happening again.

7. **Which of the following parts of speech did Mr. Sheffield's use that confused David?**
   (Average) (Skill 1.4)

   A. An improper use of an interjection

   B. An idiomatic expression

   C. A metaphorical expression

   D. A prepositional phrase

8. **Mr. Sheffield can best help David and other ELLs by using which of the following strategies?**
   (Rigorous) (Skill 4.3)

   A. Daily introduction of an idiom followed by conversation and contextual use

   B. Posters and lists of idioms posted in the classroom with other examples of parts of speech

   C. Providing articles and reading materials which use idiomatic expressions

   D. Pairing ELLs with English-speaking students and encouraging natural conversations

9. **A primary reason that activities using idioms will be effective in helping the ELLs in Mr. Sheffield's class is that this kind of practice will build their:**
   (Average) (Skill 1.4)

   A. confidence in speaking conversational English.

   B. ability to listen carefully.

   C. conversational English development.

   D. attention to visual details.

10. **By introducing idioms on a daily basis and discussing them in context, Mr. Sheffield is using which of the following type of activities?**
(Easy) (Skill 4.3)

A. Discussion

B. Participation

C. Performance

D. Linguistically structured

11. **Which of the following student activities would best support Mr. Sheffield's activity if his goal is to bring together the four strands of listening, speaking, reading, and writing?**
(Rigorous) (Skill 5.2)

A. Maintain a daily journal entry of the idiom for the day.

B. Record a variety of idiomatic expressions from daily readings by using a recording device.

C. Discuss and pantomime various idioms with an English-speaking partner.

D. Identify an idiom in a daily reading, record the idiom, and draw a picture that shows its literal and figurative meaning.

12. **Which action does a language learner perform according to Krashen's Monitor Hypothesis?**
(Rigorous) (Skill 2.1)

A. The learner relaxes and allows learning to take place.

B. The learner is highly motivated by external factors.

C. The learner has a grammar check that kicks in and corrects incorrect utterances.

D. The learner learns language naturally as a child learns a first language.

13. **Which researcher(s) theorized that "collaborative interaction in which meaning is negotiated with peers is central to the language acquisition process"?**
(Rigorous) (Skill 2.2)

A. Dulay and Burt

B. Collier

C. Bialystok

D. Vygotsky

14. **When a student empathizes with other students, she is practicing which kind of learning strategy?**
(Average) (Skill 2.3)

A. Cognitive

B. Socioaffective

C. Metacognitive

D. All of the above

15. **Overgeneralization means:**
(Easy) (Skill 2.4)

A. adding "ed" to irregular verbs as a way to use the past tense.

B. stating "I have a house beautiful in Miami" for "I have a beautiful house in Miami."

C. Hispanics pronouncing words like "student" as "estudent."

D. asking someone if "You like?" instead of "Do you like this one?"

16. **Larsen-Freeman explained the seemingly randomness of second-language learning as:**
(Easy) (Skill 2.5)

A. a U-shaped behavior.

B. Chaos theory.

C. a backsliding theory.

D. a Venn diagram

17. **ELPS is an acronym for which of the following?**
(Easy) (Skill 3.1)

A. English Language Proficiency Standards

B. English Language Primary Status

C. English Language Proficiency Score

D. English Language Preparation Skills

18. **Which one of the following is an example of shared discourse?**
(Rigorous) (Skill 3.1)

A. Playing games, for example, Simon Says

B. Researching the length of different rivers

C. Writing riddles

D. Writing poetry

19. In a second grade classroom, the teacher designed a science project about the weather. After the children observed the changing weather patterns for two weeks, they recorded their information in their science notebooks and later made a large poster in groups. This activity followed good ESOL practice because:
(Average) (Skill 3.2)

   A. background knowledge was activated.

   B. weather was part of the science curriculum.

   C. the activity represented genuine communication.

   D. All of the above

20. Which of the following techniques is used by an instructor to allow the ESL student to contribute knowledge without pressure?
(Rigorous) (Skill 3.2)

   A. Instructional conversations

   B. Chats with parents and their children

   C. Reports given by a group on a topic they researched

   D. Learning only the specific language for the task at hand

21. Which of the following activities would be considered an oral communicative activity?
(Easy) (Skill 3.3)

   A. Research

   B. A written report

   C. Teacher/student/teacher questions and answers

   D. Peer interviews

22. Mr. Salinas, a fifth grade ESL teacher, wants to help his intermediate and advanced ELLs improve their oral reading fluency. After assigning reading partners, he selects reading materials at various levels that meet the lowest reading level to the highest instructional level of his ELLs. When Mr. Salinas chooses reading materials at various levels, he understands that:
(Rigorous) (Skill 3.3)

   A. it is better if each student has a different book to ensure that all students are reading independently from a large variety of materials.

   B. the use of scaffolding meets the individual needs of ELLs while enabling them to assume responsibility for their learning.

   C. by providing texts at different levels, all students will be better able to read all the materials within a certain time frame.

   D. the state requirements for differentiation in reading materials for ELLs.

23. Which one of the following is NOT a valid reason for employing the Internet in the classroom?
(Easy) (Skill 3.4)

A. Frequent communication

B. Interesting projects

C. Timely projects

D. Release time for the teacher

24. Which of the following is one way to welcome an ELL to a new culture?
(Easy) (Skill 3.5)

A. Encourage him/her to speak.

B. Assign books to be read aloud.

C. Smile when the student is mispronouncing a word.

D. Assign a peer partner.

25. Task-based activities might include:
(Average) (Skill 4.1)

A. rapid-fire commands.

B. rearrangement of jumbled items.

C. individualized tasks and reports.

D. watching a movie.

26. Which one of the following is NOT a specific comprehension skill?
(Easy) (Skill 4.2)

A. Paraphrasing

B. Summarizing

C. Questioning

D. Expressing a wish

27. The fifth grade content-area teacher has decided to ask her students to recommend a new topic for their class to study. What would be the best strategy to use so that ELLs also participate?
(Rigorous) (Skill 4.3)

A. Have students talk with their parents about language courses they took when they were in school.

B. Suggest ideas and have students vote on the best ones.

C. Allow several days for students to investigate, and then brainstorm.

D. Group students together and have them discuss their ideas.

28. After numerous arguments and misunderstandings during recess, Mr. Smith realized that the ELLs in his fourth grade class were having difficulties in getting along with the other students. After making numerous observations, Mr. Smith found that his ELLs needed direct instruction in the use of nonverbal elements of English, such as shrugs, head nods, grimaces, and so on. Which of the following best explains why Mr. Smith needs to do this?
(Average) (Skill 4.6)

A. There are more taboos associated with English-speaking cultures than found in other cultures.

B. Gestures, without verbal clues, need to be connected to specific phrases in the new language.

C. All ELLs need explicit instruction in a culture's nonverbal communication.

D. Gestures and body language vary from one culture to another.

DIRECTIONS: Use the information below to answer the questions that follow.

Ms. Thomas teaches a high school chemistry class that consists of English-speaking students and ELLs of varying abilities. Knowing students need to review basic elements and their symbols, Ms. Thomas collects a variety of audio and online materials to support an activity that incorporates listening and speaking as students work together in small groups. During the course of the activity, Ms. Thomas overhears Arun incorrectly use a term that is pivotal to understanding a particular component of the periodic table. Ms. Thomas quietly talks with Arun, and expresses her pleasure in his response yet corrects his misunderstanding and refers him to one of the audio supports in his group. She is pleased to note that he reviewed the support and now correctly uses the term during group discussion.

29. By having students use audio and online materials to discuss and review basic elements and symbols in their groups, Ms. Thomas has:
(Average) (Skill 9.2)

A. created a task-based activity that meets the linguistic needs of her ELLs.

B. provided a culturally supportive learning environment for her students.

C. shown she understands the developmental characteristics of her ELLs.

D. created an opportunity to gather anecdotal records on Arun.

30. **When Ms. Thomas quietly talks with Arun, and expresses her pleasure in his response yet corrects his misunderstanding, she is showing that she:**
(Rigorous) (Skill 4.7)

   A. is monitoring the groups and using these opportunities to maintain a running record of each student's mastery of the subject.

   B. is aware of the importance of feedback in a positive manner.

   C. is concerned about the cultural differences between her students.

   D. understands the importance of group work for Arun's academic needs.

31. **Ms. Thomas' high school chemistry class is a model of which type of ESL program?**
(Average) (Skill 8.2)

   A. Content-based ESL

   B. Structured English immersion

   C. Self-contained

   D. Submersion with primary language support

32. **Ms. Thomas wishes to build into the activity a component that addresses strengthening her ELLs' visual recognition of the elements and symbols. Which of the following would be the best component to use?**
(Rigorous) (Skill 4.4)

   A. Students quiz each other on terms listed on the cards.

   B. Students take a culminating quiz to test what they have learned from the activity.

   C. Students organize cards of the elements and symbols into a periodic table.

   D. Students copy the elements and symbols in their science journal at the conclusion of the activity.

33. **The word *mère* in French and the word *mama* in Spanish are examples of which of the following?**
(Rigorous) (Skill 4.5)

   A. Phonemes

   B. Grapheme-phoneme relationships

   C. Cognates

   D. Morphemes

34. Which of the following options is a nonintrusive way to give feedback?
(Easy) (Skill 4.7)

A. Thumbs up

B. An explanation of the grammar rule when a mistake occurs

C. Asking the ELL's peers to correct the error

D. Repeating the errors on an error sheet and asking students to correct them

DIRECTIONS: Use the information below to answer the questions that follow.

Mr. Martinez and his first grade ELLs are discussing the events in a book that is being read aloud to the class.

Mr. M: *Why did the little boy cry in this story?*

Juanita: *He sad.*

Mr. M: *Yes Juanita! Good answer! Why is he sad?*

Juanita: *Lost dog.*

Mr. M: *Juanita, that is excellent! Yes, the little boy is sad because he lost his dog. How do you think he lost his dog?*

Juanita: *No.*

Mr. M: *It's all right that we don't know yet so let's read the rest of the story to find out the answer to that question.*

35. In looking at Mr. Martinez's interaction with Juanita, which of the following best describes his responses?
(Rigorous) (Skill 4.7)

A. Trying to develop Juanita's speaking proficiency

B. Increasing Juanita's reading comprehension through reading aloud

C. Correcting Juanita's use of English in her responses

D. Using appropriate feedback to encourage Juanita's participation

36. Based on Juanita's responses, what is her speaking proficiency level?
(Average) (Skill 7.3)

A. Beginning

B. Intermediate

C. Advanced

D. Advanced high

37. **Mr. Martinez's use of positive feedback and relaxed discussion with Juanita best supports which of the following?**
(Average) (Skill 6.4)

   A. Cognitive processes toward reading comprehension

   B. Creating a positive affective filter for Juanita

   C. Increasing social abilities in speaking

   D. Activating background knowledge to make cognitive connections

38. **A high school English teacher is preparing a vocabulary lesson for her ESL class, based on a book that they will read. The best way for the teacher to introduce a word to students is to:**
(Average) (Skill 5.1)

   A. show students its dictionary definition and discuss its article of speech.

   B. create a list of its synonyms and antonyms.

   C. present the word in a variety of sentences and have students derive its meaning through context clues.

   D. use the students' native language to define the word and use it in its context from the book.

39. **Which of the following would be an appropriate writing task for beginning ELLs?**
(Average) (Skill 5.2)

   A. Reading the school menu and marking the ELL's choices

   B. Taking notes on the daily activities into a class notebook

   C. Copying a note inviting parents to a school meeting

   D. Writing a letter to the editor of the school newspaper

40. **Ms. Ray is working with a second grade student who is considered a beginning ELL. She has letters on the table that spell the word *cat*. She has the student sound out the word by saying the sound of each letter. Ms. Ray then has the student read the word. She repeats this with the words *hat* and *mat*. Ms. Ray is developing the student's ability to do which of the following?**
(Rigorous) (Skill 5.3)

   A. Repeated readings of high-frequency words

   B. Sight word reading practice

   C. Phoneme-grapheme correspondence

   D. Reading of phonetically irregular words

41. Which one of the following is a way to help a student remember information?
(Average) (Skill 5.4)

A. Establishing the purpose of the experiment

B. Recording information

C. Studying headings and subheadings

D. Creating artwork

42. Ms. Ochoa is planning the vocabulary introduction to the new unit on Space in her middle school ELL science class. During her planning, she has created the following steps to follow for student understanding of the unit vocabulary:

- Teacher gives a description, explanation, or example for each word.
- Students restate or explain each word's meaning in their own words.
- Students create a picture or graphic for each word.
- Students discuss the terms with one another.

However, Ms. Ochoa felt that another step needed to be added in order to help ELLs create connections with prior knowledge of the terms being learned in this unit. Ms. Ochoa could:
(Rigorous) (Skill 5.5)

A. involve students in games that allow them to play with the vocabulary for this unit.

B. have students write the vocabulary and terms in a journal, including definitions and use in a sentence.

C. provide students with numerous print and media materials on the subject that re-enforce vocabulary and terms.

D. encourage students to create a content map in their native language (that also incorporates English terms) showing what they already know.

43. An English teacher included a unit on fairy tales in her classroom. To promote critical literacy, she could have her students:
(Average) (Skill 5.6)

A. provide a list of prereading questions for discussion.

B. use a flowchart to outline the different plots.

C. compare the stories with their native-language versions.

D. make cartoon drawings illustrating the stories.

44. **Mr. Hardy teaches a fourth grade ESL class. Knowing that his students come from a variety of backgrounds and development levels, he creates a game in which teams of students work at identifying common, everyday signs and text, such as menus, road signs, and so on. He expects students to respond in English, supporting each other in their teams. Based on this activity, Mr. Hardy is helping his ELL students to develop which skill?**
(Rigorous)(Skill 5.6)

A. Association with everyday written items

B. Basic literacy skill of writing

C. A unified understanding of language

D. Connections between everyday items

45. **Which one of the following has an impact on the literacy of an L2 student?**
(Rigorous) (Skill 5.7)

A. Familial literacy

B. Parents who read to their child

C. Parents involved in the child's schooling

D. All of the above

46. **Which one of the following is a CALP?**
(Rigorous) (Skill 6.1)

A. Review Chapter 1 for tomorrow's test.

B. Good morning.

C. Nice to meet you.

D. All of the above

47. **Keeping a learning log is an example of which of the following integrated approaches to language teaching?**
(Easy) (Skill 6.2)

A. Graphic organizer

B. Task-based or experiential learning

C. Cooperative learning

D. Whole-language approach

48. **Which one of the following is NOT an advantage of learning and using more than one language?**
(Average) (Skill 6.3)

A. Cognitive rigidity

B. Increased visual-social abilities

C. More logical reasoning skills

D. Better problem-solving and analytical skills

49. Which one of the following is NOT an instance of instrumental motivation in language learning? *(Rigorous) (Skill 6.4)*

A. Moving to a different country or into another culture

B. Getting a job that requires speaking in a different language

C. Parents enrolling their child in a foreign language class

D. Desiring to communicate with other peoples and learn about their culture

50. Which of the following is NOT an attribute of a viable test for ELLs? *(Average) (Skill 7.1)*

A. Reliable

B. Valid

C. Cost-effective

D. Practical

51. A middle school language arts teacher has a group of ELLs who have varying degrees of English-language abilities. While planning how to assess students' progress she relies on which of the following? *(Rigorous) (Skill 7.2)*

A. Test scores that reflect the whole school population

B. The use of a bell curve to plot students' results and progress

C. Assessment results only in the areas of English in which they have achieved mastery

D. Observations, test scores, and samples of daily work

52. Before the 2013–14 school year began, Ms. Rawlins took the time to look at the test scores of her incoming ELL Spanish-speaking sixth grade students. She noted that several of her ELLs took a modified STAAR test due to their language, but not because of a learning disability. Which of the following tests would they have taken? *(Easy) (Skill 7.3)*

A. STAAR L

B. STAAR Modified

C. STAAR Spanish

D. STAAR Alternate

53. An ESL teacher at a local middle school had to determine if an ELL needed to be retained. Which of the following standardized assessments should the teacher NOT take into consideration when making this decision?
(Rigorous) (Skills 7.3, 7.5)

A. TELPAS

B. Previous TAKS scores (implemented before STAAR)

C. STAAR

D. All of the above

54. According to the definition of LEPs in Title VII, which one of the following statements about LEPs is NOT applicable?
(Average) (Skill 7.4)

A. The student is a native American or Alaska native.

B. The student not born in the United States.

C. The student is migratory.

D. The student gas little difficulty with English.

55. Before the school year began, Ms. Davilla decided to look through her fifth grade ELL records from the previous year. She wanted to know how her students performed on the final writing exam. In reviewing their scores, Ms. Davilla should look at which of the following to fully understand what skills her students mastered?
(Rigorous) (Skill 7.5)

A. The final, overall writing score

B. The individually mastered TEKS

C. What modifications were used

D. The prompt that was given for the writing assignment

56. Which one of the following is a way that teachers can NOT use the information gathered in testing?
(Rigorous) (Skill 7.6)

A. To improve their teaching

B. To demonstrate a special needs student's deficiencies

C. To orient their teaching practices in more desirable ways

D. To plan remedial work

57. Which of the following is NOT a requirement for schools to meet based on the Lau Plan (*Lau* v. *Nichols*)?
(Average) (Skill 8.1)

A. Provide all students with the same textbooks, teachers, and curriculums

B. Identify assessments and evaluative tools for ongoing assessment

C. Form and convene a Language Proficiency Assessment Committee (LPAC)

D. Outline specific staff responsibilities and credentials for instruction

58. The No Child Left Behind (NCLB) Act does NOT require schools to:
(Rigorous) (Skill 8.1)

A. give assessment in English if the LEP has received three years of schooling in the U.S. (except for Puerto Rico).

B. measure school districts by status.

C. inform parents of the school's evaluation.

D. increase the length of the school year.

59. Which one of the following methods aims for English proficiency?
(Rigorous) (Skill 8.2)

A. Canadian French Immersion Program

B. Indigenous language immersion programs

C. Structured English immersion

D. Submersion with primary language support

60. At a local elementary school, there has been a large influx of bilingual and ESL Spanish-speaking students in the primary grades. Based on the sudden change in population, the school's administration needs to make management decisions on available resources based on which of the following?
(Average) (Skill 8.3)

A. District demographics

B. Student characteristics

C. District resources

D. School resources

61. Which of the following instructional approaches emphasizes LEPs' acquiring new language skills through the content areas?
(Average) (Skills 5.6, 8.4)

A. TPR

B. Natural Approach

C. CALLA

D. Communicative Approach

62. Ms. Wilson asked her students to act as translators during recent family conferences. In one instance, the father looked increasingly anxious as he struggled to make himself understood. What went wrong?
(Average) (Skill 9.1)

A. The father was insulted by the situation.

B. The ELL was a good student and translated the teacher's comments well.

C. The ELL was reluctant to translate.

D. The father was proud of his son's/daughter's skill.

63. Mr. Sanchez, a new ESOL instructor, wanted to establish a highly effective learning classroom for his students. Which of the following would be conducive to his goal?
(Average) (Skill 9.2)

A. Lots of educational technology

B. A large classroom library

C. Textbooks of different reading levels

D. All of the above

64. Which one of the following actions will help an ELL adjust to a new school and provide a positive learning environment?
(Average) (Skill 9.3)

A. Placing the ELL in a group of all English speakers

B. Calling on the newcomer frequently to make him/her feel like part of the class

C. Assigning a classmate to guide him/her through essential routines

D. Urging the newcomer to tell the class about his/her homeland

65. **Which of the following is a reason to offer classroom lectures instead of cooperative group work?** *(Easy) (Skill 9.4)*

    A. They increase student concentration.

    B. Students learn better.

    C. The teacher is seen as an academic authority.

    D. Group work is unproductive.

66. **A teacher who decides that her ELLs are lazy and indifferent to learning about U.S. culture is guilty of which of the following?** *(Rigorous) (Skills 9.3, 9.5)*

    A. Racism

    B. Stereotyping

    C. Discrimination

    D. Ethnocentrism

67. **At the beginning of the school year, the ESL teacher provided parents with information on the services offered at the local library in their native language. The information covered online resources, free language classes, and after-school tutoring. It is obvious that the ESL teacher understands the importance of which of the following?** *(Rigorous) (Skill 10.1)*

    A. Collaborating effectively with parents and guardians of ELL students

    B. Communicating general information about English and English-language instruction

    C. Facilitating participation in school activities

    D. Advocating educational and social equity for ELLs

68. **The majority of ELLs in Mr. Sosa's ESL class lack basic technology in the home. Wanting to develop computer literacy in his students, Mr. Sosa implements an evening class in the computer lab for students and their family members on using the Internet and district databases as a means of supporting classroom lessons. Mr. Sosa also sets aside a time once a week during the day for parents to come in and use the computer lab to access their children's online records and classwork. Based on this information, it is obvious that Mr. Sosa understands:**
   (Rigorous) (Skill 10.2)

   A. the importance of family involvement in their child's learning.

   B. that advocating for ELLs will ensure their participation in learning.

   C. that it is important to communicate and collaborate with school personnel about the use of school resources.

   D. the importance of encouraging constructive use of students' time while at school.

69. **Which one of the following is the best reason for encouraging outreach programs in which family members are involved in school activities?**
   (Average) (Skill 10.3)

   A. The program provides extra support for students.

   B. Parents can provide discipline for their children.

   C. Parents learn life skills for the new country.

   D. It's easier to ask for additional resources directly from parents.

70. **Which one of the following points is the most important reason for inviting speakers from the ELLs' community to the classroom?**
   (Average) (Skill 10.4)

   A. Increasing students' knowledge

   B. Motivating ELLs to succeed

   C. Advocating for increased funding

   D. Encouraging good student behavior

SAMPLE TEST 1 ANSWER KEY AND RIGOR TABLE

Sample Test 1 Answer Key

1. C	11. D	21. D	31. C	41. D	51. D	61. C
2. D	12. C	22. B	32. C	42. D	52. A	62. A
3. A	13. B	23. D	33. C	43. C	53. A	63. D
4. B	14. B	24. D	34. A	44. A	54. D	64. C
5. C	15. A	25. B	35. D	45. D	55. B	65. C
6. D	16. B	26. D	36. A	46. A	56. B	66. B
7. B	17. A	27. D	37. B	47. D	57. A	67. D
8. A	18. A	28. D	38. C	48. A	58. D	68. A
9. C	19. D	29. A	39. C	49. D	59. C	69. A
10. D	20. A	30. B	40. C	50. C	60. D	70. B

Sample Test 1 Rigor Table

Rigor Level	Questions
Easy (20%)	5, 6, 10, 15, 16, 17, 21, 23, 24, 26, 34, 47, 52, 65
Average (40%)	1, 3, 4, 7, 9, 14, 19, 25, 28, 29, 31, 36, 37, 38, 39, 41, 43, 48, 50, 54, 57, 60, 61, 62, 63, 64, 69, 70
Rigorous (40%)	2, 8, 11, 12, 13, 18, 20, 22, 27, 30, 32, 33, 35, 40, 42, 44, 45, 46, 49, 51, 53, 55, 56, 58, 59, 66, 67, 68

SAMPLE TEST 1 ANSWERS WITH RATIONALES

1. **Language learners seem to acquire language by which process?**
(Average) (Skill 1.1)

   A. A different process from learning in general

   B. A slower process than how they acquire their native tongue

   C. A gradual, hierarchical, and cumulative process

   D. A random process

   Answer: C. A gradual, hierarchical, and cumulative process
   All language learners must go through the same hierarchical steps in their language learning process. They advance from the least to the most complicated stage regardless of whether it is in the L1 or L2. The process is very similar to learning in general, and language learners progress more rapidly through the stages than when learning their native language.

2. **Mr. White's fourth grade ELLs are working in groups with native English-language speakers. The purpose of the activity is to have students: (1) identify root words and their meanings, and (2) see how prefixes alter the meanings of root words. Which of the following best describes Mr. White's thought in using this activity?**
(Rigorous) (Skill 1.1)

   A. Knows the functions and registers of language and uses this knowledge to develop and modify instruction for ELLs

   B. Understands how listening, speaking, reading, and writing develops the ELL's English language proficiency

   C. Knows the benefits of having students work in groups

   D. Understands the importance of students learning the basic concepts of the English language

   Answer: D. Understands the importance of students learning the basic concepts of the English language
   Mr. White knows that the key to understanding a word is to identify the root or base word and any subsequent change due to prefixes or suffixes. Option A is not correct because this activity does not address the functions and registers of the English language, such as the difference between academic and social registers. Option B is incorrect as this activity is not a situation in which instruction is focused on all four of these learning aspects. Option C is not correct because while students are working in groups, the lesson's focus is on understanding root words and the changes in their meaning when adding a prefix or suffix.

DIRECTIONS: Use the information below to answer the questions that follow.

In her fourth grade ESL class, Ms. Nelson had her students answer a prompt that required them to write three. The following is a paragraph written by Ishmael, one of her ELLs:

When Billy go two the store, he red a add for a sail on hot dogs. He buy 2. And eight them right then. He new he would be in trouble if his ant finds out. Becuz she is making a specail dinner. Billy leaves. He walked home.

3. **Based on Ishmael's writing sample, Ms. Nelson knew that she had to reteach which of the following English conventions?**
(Average) (Skill 1.1)

   A. Homophones

   B. Phonographemic differences

   C. Homonyms

   D. Homographs

Answer: A. Homophones
Ishmael's writing sample shows his confusion over selecting the correct word. *Homophones* are words that have the same pronunciation, but different meanings and spellings. *Phonographemic differences* encompass not just homophones, but also homonyms and homographs. *Homonyms* is a general term for a group of words that are spelled and sound alike or words that are spelled the same, but have two or more meanings. *Homographs* are spelled the same, but they have different meanings.

4. **Ms. Nelson plans to reteach homophones to her class, targeting the use of visual aids, such as illustrations, to show differences between homophones as well as using the words in sentences during discussions. Based on Ms. Nelson's plans, it is obvious that she is using which of the following adaptations?**
(Average) (Skill 3.2)

   A. Nonverbal

   B. Contextual

   C. Paraverbal

   D. Discourse

Answer: B. Contextual
Ms. Nelson is using visual aids and an auditory component to strengthen the differences between the targeted homophones. Option A is not correct as a nonverbal adaptation addresses gestures and facial expressions. Option C requires teachers to speak more clearly and use volume and intonation to convey meaning. Option D is not correct as discourse adaptations are based on verbal markers such as "now" and "first" to make what they say more comprehensible.

5. **Ms. Nelson also decides that, based on Ishmael's writing, there needs to be further work on which of the following?**
(Easy) (Skill 1.3)

A. Complex sentence structure

B. Use of compound sentences

C. Creating a simple sentence

D. Use of a compound predicate

Answer: C. Creating a simple sentence
Option C is the correct answer because it is evident that Ishmael writes incomplete sentences. Therefore, options A, B, and D cannot be correct.

6. **Changes in register are a result of which of the following sociolinguistic factors?**
(Rigorous) (Skill 1.2)

A. The person to whom one is speaking

B. Knowledge of the topic

C. Attitude toward the listeners

D. All of the above

Answer: D. All of the above
Changes in register are related to all of the listed sociolinguistic factors: the person to whom one is speaking, knowledge of the topic, and attitude toward the listeners.

DIRECTIONS: Use the information below to answer the questions that follow.

Mr. Sheffield wants to focus on developing students' speaking skills, so he engages his students in a discussion with his ESL class as to how their spring break was. During the discussion, all the students were comfortable participating and listening to each other. A portion of the discussion is shown below.

Mr. S: *I'm so pleased that so many of you had such a great spring break! Maria, what did you do over spring break?*

Maria: *My abuelita, my grandmother, came to visit. We had fun.*

Mr. S: *That sounds wonderful! I am sure you were happy to see her. David, what about you? How was your spring break?*

David: *I was sick most of the time.*

Mr. S: *I am so sorry that you were under the weather! That is not a good way to spend your vacation.*

At Mr. Sheffield's response, David looked confused and stopped participating in the discussion. While Mr. Sheffield noticed David's withdrawal, he continued the discussion before beginning the lesson. At the end of the class period, Mr. Sheffield took a few moments to speak with David and, at that point, David explained that he did not know what Mr. Sheffield meant by saying that David was *under the weather.* Mr. Sheffield realized his mistake, corrected it, and began to plan a strategy that would prevent this from happening again.

7. **Which of the following parts of speech did Mr. Sheffield's use that confused David?**
(Average) (Skill 1.4)

   A. An improper use of an interjection

   B. An idiomatic expression

   C. A metaphorical expression

   D. A prepositional phrase

   Answer: B. An idiomatic expression
   Option B is the correct answer. Idiomatic expressions are very problematic for ELLs, yet they are a part of American conversational speech and writing. An idiom is a natural way of speaking to a native speaker of the language. Options A, C, and D are not correct as Mr. Sheffield did not misuse any of these.

8. **Mr. Sheffield can best help David and other ELLs by using which of the following strategies?**
(Rigorous) (Skill 4.3)

   A. Daily introduction of an idiom followed by conversation and contextual use

   B. Posters and lists of idioms posted in the classroom with other examples of parts of speech

   C. Providing articles and reading materials which use idiomatic expressions

   D. Pairing ELLs with English-speaking students and encouraging natural conversations

   Answer: A. Daily introduction of an idioms followed by conversation and contextual use
   Through the use of structured discussion, contextual support, and introduction of idioms on a daily basis, ELLs will be able to accurately identify the idiom and its meaning within daily conversations and readings. Option B is not correct as only having visual materials will not foster an internalization of an idiom's meaning. Option C is incorrect because providing reading materials will not provide verbal contextual support. Option D is not correct because encouraging conversations does not guarantee the use of idioms or their meaning.

9. **A primary reason that activities using idioms will be effective in helping the ELLs in Mr. Sheffield's class is that this kind of practice will build their:**
(Average) (Skill 1.4)

   A. confidence in speaking conversational English.

   B. ability to listen carefully.

   C. conversational English development.

   D. attention to visual details.

Answer: C. conversational English development

Idiomatic expressions are a natural part of conversational English that can often prove problematic for ELLs. By recognizing and learning idiomatic expressions, students develop fluency in speaking with their peers. Option A is incorrect because learning idiomatic expressions is a development process that once mastered leads toward a confidence in listening and speaking. Option B is not correct as conversation will help build mastery with idioms rather than just listening. Option D is incorrect, although using visual materials will help support conversational use of idioms.

10. **By introducing idioms on a daily basis and discussing them in context, Mr. Sheffield is using which of the following type of activities?**
(Easy) (Skill 4.3)

A. Discussion

B. Participation

C. Performance

D. Linguistically structured

Answer: D. Linguistically structured

Mr. Sheffield is utilizing a controlled, repetitive activity that incorporates structure yet also incorporates discussion in order to introduce his students to a part of speech in the English language. Option A is not correct as discussion activities are opportunities for ELLs to speak, share, and listen at their current state of ability. Option B is not correct. While students are participating, it would not be within a structured learning format. Option C is incorrect as students are not performing nor presenting a pre-developed message.

11. **Which of the following student activities would best support Mr. Sheffield's activity if his goal is to bring together the four strands of listening, speaking, reading, and writing?**
(Rigorous) (Skill 5.2)

A. Maintain a daily journal entry of the idiom for the day.

B. Record a variety of idiomatic expressions from daily readings by using a recording device.

C. Discuss and pantomime various idioms with an English-speaking partner.

D. Identify an idiom in a daily reading, record the idiom, and draw a picture that shows its literal and figurative meaning.

Answer: D. Identify an idiom in a daily reading, record the idiom, and draw a picture that shows its literal and figurative meaning

Mr. Sheffield's activity incorporates two strands, listening and speaking. By locating the idiom in a reading, writing the idiom, and subsequently drawing its literal and figurative meaning, students are internalizing the idiom's meaning within the four strands of learning. Option A brings in only one strand, writing. Option B brings in only one strand, reading.

Option C is not correct as it supports Mr. Sheffield's original activity that incorporates two strands.

12. Which action does a language learner perform according to Krashen's Monitor Hypothesis?
(Rigorous) (Skill 2.1)

   A. The learner relaxes and allows learning to take place.

   B. The learner is highly motivated by external factors.

   C. The learner has a grammar check that kicks in and corrects incorrect utterances.

   D. The learner learns language naturally as a child learns a first language.

Answer: C. The learner has a grammar check that kicks in and corrects incorrect utterances
According to the Monitor Hypothesis, a language learner monitors his or her learning. Option A refers to Krashen's affective filter. Option B refers to the types of motivation to which a learner is subjected. Option D refers to natural acquisition as compared with the formal learning of an adult.

13. Which researcher(s) theorized that "collaborative interaction in which meaning is negotiated with peers is central to the language acquisition process"?
(Rigorous) (Skill 2.2)

   A. Dulay and Burt

   B. Collier

   C. Bialystok

   D. Vygotsky

Answer: B. Collier
Virginia Collier's research suggested that highly interactive classes are likely to provide the kind of social setting for natural language acquisition to take place simultaneously with academic and cognitive development. Dulay and Burt argued that the frequency of certain items in the target language appear to contribute to output. Bialystok found that cognitive and academic development in the first language affects schooling in L2. Vygotsky's work focused on the relationship between development of thought and language.

14. When a student empathizes with other students, she is practicing which kind of learning strategy? *(Average) (Skill 2.3)*

A. Cognitive

B. Socioaffective

C. Metacognitive

D. All of the above

Answer: B. Socioaffective
All students are required to practice cognitive, metacognitive, and socioaffective learning strategies to become good learners. By empathizing with another student or students, the learner is practicing socioaffective strategies where she understands a fellow student and so helps herself also.

15. Overgeneralization means: *(Easy) (Skill 2.4)*

A. adding "ed" to irregular verbs as a way to use the past tense.

B. stating "I have a house beautiful in Miami" for "I have a beautiful house in Miami."

C. Hispanics pronouncing words like "student" as "estudent."

D. asking someone if "You like?" instead of "Do you like this one?"

Answer: A. adding "ed" to irregular verbs as a way to use the past tense
Simplification is a common learner error involving simplifying the language when the correct structures have not been internalized as shown in Option D. Options B and C are examples of L1 transfer to L2. Option A is the correct answer as it demonstrates how the learner attempts to apply a rule learned without regard for irregular verbs in English.

16. Larsen-Freeman explained the seemingly randomness of second-language learning as: *(Easy) (Skill 2.5)*

A. a U-shaped behavior.

B. Chaos theory.

C. a backsliding theory.

D. a Venn diagram.

Answer: B. Chaos theory
Interlanguage occurs when the second-language learner lacks proficiency in L2 and tries to compensate for his or her lack of fluency in the new language. This may be interpreted using Option D, a Venn diagram. The backsliding theory, or U-shaped behavior, was used by Long to explain the contradictions of second-language acquisition. Larsen-Freeman used the Chaos theory.

17. ELPS is an acronym for which of the following?
(Easy) (Skill 3.1)

A. English Language Proficiency Standards

B. English Language Primary Status

C. English Language Proficiency Score

D. English Language Preparation Skills

Answer: A. English Language Proficiency Standards
The ELPS provides descriptors of the levels used to determine an ELL's English-language proficiency. Options B, C, and D are not correct.

18. Which one of the following is an example of shared discourse?
(Rigorous) (Skill 3.1)

A. Playing games, for example, Simon Says

B. Researching the length of different rivers

C. Writing riddles

D. Writing poetry

Answer: A. Playing games, for example, Simon Says
There are four major types of discourse: shared discourse, fun discourse, fact discourse, and thought discourse. Shared discourse is the area of discourse in which language is used to socially communicate and share meaning in order to accomplish social goals

(playing games or planning a short scene).

19. In a second grade classroom, the teacher designed a science project about the weather. After the children observed the changing weather patterns for two weeks, they recorded their information in their science notebooks and later made a large poster in groups. This activity followed good ESOL practice because:
(Average) (Skill 3.2)

A. background knowledge was activated.

B. weather was part of the science curriculum.

C. the activity represented genuine communication.

D. All of the above

Answer: D. All of the above
Since weather is part of daily life, it activated background knowledge in learners. In addition, because weather is part of the science curriculum, the activity used words from the content area to also activate background knowledge. Finally, children communicated what they had learned thereby creating real communication in the classroom.

20. Which of the following techniques is used by an instructor to allow the ESL student to contribute knowledge without pressure? *(Rigorous) (Skill 3.2)*

A. Instructional conversations

B. Chats with parents and their children

C. Reports given by a group on a topic they researched

D. Learning only the specific language for the task at hand

Answer: A. Instructional conversations
Options B and D may be discarded since they may both contribute to a student's anxiety. Option C may be difficult for those students who are not comfortable in front of a group. Only Option A is a way in which the teacher can develop a rapport with the student through eliciting more information in an extended conversation with a student.

21. Which of the following activities would be considered an oral communicative activity? *(Easy) (Skill 3.3)*

A. Research

B. A written report

C. Teacher/student/teacher questions and answers

D. Peer interviews

Answer: D. Peer interviews
Communicative activities are activities in which both parties gain meaningful insights into the topic at hand: problem-solving conversations, debates, or peer interviews, for example. Teacher/student/teacher questions and answers do not. They are ways in which the teacher controls the "communication" and learning activity—little is gained—or learned—by either party. Options A and B are written communicative activities. Option D is an oral communicative activity.

22. Mr. Salinas, a fifth grade ESL teacher, wants to help his intermediate and advanced ELLs improve their oral reading fluency. After assigning reading partners, he selects reading materials at various levels that meet the lowest reading level to the highest instructional level of his ELLs. When Mr. Salinas chooses reading materials at various levels, he understands that:
(Rigorous) (Skill 3.3)

A. it is better if each student has a different book to ensure that all students are reading independently from a large variety of materials.

B. the use of scaffolding meets the individual needs of ELLs while enabling them to assume responsibility for their learning.

C. by providing texts at different levels, all students will be better able to read all the materials within a certain time frame.

D. the state requirements for differentiation in reading materials for ELLs.

Answer: B. the use of scaffolding meets the individual needs of ELLs while enabling them to assume responsibility for their learning
Providing intermediate and advanced ELLs with scaffolded texts enables students to select texts at their independent level. Students have opportunities to increase fluency through numerous rereadings of texts that they are successful with, thus increasing desire to continue to improve their fluency. Option A is not correct as Mr. Salinas' goal for fluency is for students to work together, not independently. Option C is not correct as intermediate ELLs will not be successful at the same reading level nor in the same time frame as advanced ELLs. Option D is not correct as there are no state requirements to differentiate ELL reading materials during fluency practice.

23. Which one of the following is NOT a valid reason for employing the Internet in the classroom?
(Easy) (Skill 3.4)

A. Frequent communication

B. Interesting projects

C. Timely projects

D. Release time for the teacher

Answer: D. Release time for the teacher
Options A, B, and C—frequent communication and interesting and timely projects—are all valid reasons to engage children in using the Internet; Option D, creating release time for the teacher, is not.

24. Which of the following is one way to welcome an ELL to a new culture?
(Easy) (Skill 3.5)

A. Encourage him/her to speak.

B. Assign books to be read aloud.

C. Smile when the student is mispronouncing a word.

D. Assign a peer partner.

Answer D. Assign a peer partner
Although options A, B, and C each have a place in the classroom, for students struggling with a new language and culture, they may be very threatening and should not be used with newcomers.

25. Task-based activities might include:
(Average) (Skill 4.1)

A. rapid-fire commands.

B. rearrangement of jumbled items.

C. individualized tasks and reports.

D. watching a movie.

Answer: B. rearrangement of jumbled items
In rearranging items, members of a group negotiate meaning. Option A is a Total Physical Response (TPR) activity which can be done slowly as a beginning activity for ELLs. As they begin to understand spoken English and the game, TPR can be spiced up by more rapid commands. Option C defeats the purpose of task-based activities, which require the members of a group to perform together. Option D is performed individually, but it could be a prelude to further group activities.

26. Which one of the following is NOT a specific comprehension skill?
(Easy) (Skill 4.2)

A. Paraphrasing

B. Summarizing

C. Questioning

D. Expressing a wish

Answer: D. Expressing a wish
Options A, B, and C are specific comprehension skills. Unless the ELL is specifically asked to express a wish, Option D is not a specific comprehension skill.

27. The fifth grade content-area teacher has decided to ask her students to recommend a new topic for their class to study. What would be the best strategy to use so that ELLs also participate?
(Rigorous) (Skill 4.3)

A. Have students talk with their parents about language courses they took when they were in school.

B. Suggest ideas and have students vote on the best ones.

C. Allow several days for students to investigate, and then brainstorm.

D. Group students together and have them discuss their ideas.

Answer: D. Group students together and have them discuss their ideas
When students are grouped, it lessens the pressure of performing for the entire class. By discussing ideas in a group, students are given the chance to use language as they would in a natural context. Even the less skilled ELLs can contribute ideas, and peers can help them acquire more language skills. Often animated discussion occurs when students are motivated to talk about something that really interests them.

28. After numerous arguments and misunderstandings during recess, Mr. Smith realized that the ELLs in his fourth grade class were having difficulties in getting along with the other students. After making numerous observations, Mr. Smith found that his ELLs needed direct instruction in the use of nonverbal elements of English, such as shrugs, head nods, grimaces, and so on. Which of the following best explains why Mr. Smith needs to do this?
(Average) (Skill 4.6)

A. There are more taboos associated with English-speaking cultures than found in other cultures.

B. Gestures, without verbal clues, need to be connected to specific phrases in the new language.

C. All ELLs need explicit instruction in a culture's nonverbal communication.

D. Gestures and body language vary from one culture to another.

Answer: D. Gestures and body language vary from one culture to another
Option D is correct because ELLs may not fully understand nonverbal aspects of a language without direct instruction. Option A is incorrect as English does not necessarily have more than other cultures. Option B is not correct as nonverbal cues are independent of speaking. Option C is also incorrect because not all ELLs need to be explicitly taught about a culture's nonverbal communication.

Ms. Thomas teaches a high school chemistry class that consists of English-speaking students and ELLs of varying abilities. Knowing students need to review basic elements and their symbols, Ms. Thomas collects a variety of audio and online materials to support an activity that incorporates listening and speaking as students work together in small groups. During the course of the activity, Ms. Thomas overhears Arun incorrectly use a term that is pivotal to understanding a particular component of the periodic table. Ms. Thomas quietly talks with Arun, and expresses her pleasure in his response yet corrects his misunderstanding and refers him to one of the audio supports in his group. She is pleased to note that he reviewed the support and now correctly uses the term during group discussion.

29. **By having students use audio and online materials to discuss and review basic elements and symbols in their groups, Ms. Thomas has:** *(Average) (Skill 9.2)*

    A. created a task-based activity that meets the linguistic needs of her ELLs.

    B. provided a culturally supportive learning environment for her students.

    C. shown she understands the developmental characteristics of her ELLs.

    D. created an opportunity to gather anecdotal records on Arun.

Answer: A. created a task-based activity that meets the linguistic needs of her ELLs
Option A incorporates audio materials that support the linguistic needs of the ELLs in a task-based activity that is structured in a supportive group environment. Option B is not correct because using audio and online materials in the activity do not target a specific culture or specific cultural needs. Also, while Ms. Thomas may understand the development characteristics of her ELLs, in this activity she is addressing their linguistics needs therefore option C is also incorrect. Option D is not correct as her purpose is to strengthen the listening and speaking of her students, not to focus on one student in particular.

30. When Ms. Thomas quietly talks with Arun, and expresses her pleasure in his response yet corrects his misunderstanding, she is showing that she:
(Rigorous) (Skill 4.7)

A. is monitoring the groups and using these opportunities to maintain a running record of each student's mastery of the subject.

B. is aware of the importance of feedback in a positive manner.

C. is concerned about the cultural differences between her students.

D. understands the importance of group work for Arun's academic needs.

Answer: B. is aware of the importance of feedback in a positive manner
Many factors affect students' learning. By supporting his attempts in a positive yet personal way aside from the group, Ms. Thomas is giving support and recognizing his effort which, in turn, will encourage Arun's continual positive participation as is evident in his actions after her intervention. Option A is not correct as there is no indication in the scenario that Ms. Thomas is using this activity as a source for anecdotal monitoring. Option C is incorrect as no evidence is given that she has put into place strategies to offset cultural differences. Option D is not correct as her focus is on the whole class, not just one student.

31. Ms. Thomas' high school chemistry class is a model of which type of ESL program?
(Average) (Skill 8.2)

A. Content-based ESL

B. Structured English immersion

C. Self-contained

D. Submersion with primary language support

Answer: C. Self-contained
Ms. Thomas provides instructions in English to a class that is a mixture of English-speaking students and ELLs. Plus, Ms. Thomas exhibits the use of ESL methods to support the students' acquisition of the subject matter. Option A is not correct as content-based ESL is a component of an ESL pull-out program that focuses on the all-around development of a student's English acquisition. Option B is not correct as a structured English immersion is often a pull-out program with a large population of students who share the same first language. Option D is incorrect as it is obvious that Ms. Thomas' class is a mixture of ELLs and English-speaking students, and Ms. Thomas is providing the information in English.

32. Ms. Thomas wishes to build into the activity a component that addresses strengthening her ELLs' visual recognition of the elements and symbols. Which of the following would be the best component to use?
(Rigorous) (Skill 4.4)

A. Students quiz each other on terms listed on the cards.

B. Students take a culminating quiz to test what they have learned from the activity.

C. Students organize cards of the elements and symbols into a periodic table.

D. Students copy the elements and symbols in their science journal at the conclusion of the activity.

Answer: C. Students organize cards of the elements and symbols into a periodic table
Manipulating cards into a structured form provides a connection with the abstract through concrete application. ELLs have an opportunity to connect listening, speaking, and visual skills to understanding the subject. Option A, while visual, does not provide students with the opportunity to manipulate and create the diagram that they must learn. This would not provide ELLs with the visual support needed for mastery of content. Option B supports the speaking and listening component of the activity and would not be an additional component to strengthen the ELL's mastery of the review. Option D, while written, is a rote form of learning that is not the best component to add to the group activity.

33. The word *mère* in French and the word *mama* in Spanish are examples of which of the following?
(Rigorous) (Skill 4.5)

A. Phonemes

B. Grapheme-phoneme relationships

C. Cognates

D. Morphemes

Answer: C. Cognates
Phoneme refers to the smallest unit of sound that affects meaning. A *morpheme* is the smallest unit of a language system that has meaning; the units are more commonly known as the root word, prefix, and suffix. Words that mean the same in two different languages and have similar origins and spellings are called *cognates* or true cognates. Words that look similar but have different meanings are false cognates.

34. Which of the following options is a nonintrusive way to give feedback? *(Easy) (Skill 4.7)*

   A. Thumbs up

   B. An explanation of the grammar rule when a mistake occurs

   C. Asking the ELL's peers to correct the error

   D. Repeating the errors on an error sheet and asking students to correct them

Answer: A. Thumbs up
Sometimes, the smallest gesture is the easiest and most effective. Option A gives immediate feedback. Options B, C, and D take far more time and are probably not as effective.

DIRECTIONS: Use the information below to answer the questions that follow.

Mr. Martinez and his first grade ELLs are discussing the events in a book that is being read aloud to the class.

Mr. M: *Why did the little boy cry in this story?*

Juanita: *He sad.*

Mr. M: *Yes Juanita! Good answer! Why is he sad?*

Juanita: *Lost dog.*

Mr. M: *Juanita, that is excellent! Yes, the little boy is sad because he lost his dog. How do you think he lost his dog?*

Juanita: *No.*

Mr. M: *It's all right that we don't know yet so let's read the rest of the story to find out the answer to that question.*

35. In looking at Mr. Martinez's interaction with Juanita, which of the following best describes his responses? *(Rigorous) (Skill 4.7)*

   A. Trying to develop Juanita's speaking proficiency

   B. Increasing Juanita's reading comprehension through reading aloud

   C. Correcting Juanita's use of English in her responses

   D. Using appropriate feedback to encourage Juanita's participation

Answer: D. Using appropriate feedback to encourage Juanita's participation
Mr. Martinez is encouraging Juanita to answer and is providing positive feedback each time. Option A is incorrect because this discussion is not the proper format for developing speaking proficiency, which usually incorporates aspects that are familiar to the ELL. Option B is not correct, based on the discussion that is presented. Option C is incorrect because Mr. Martinez is not correcting Juanita's responses at the point of discussion.

36. Based on Juanita's responses, what is her speaking proficiency level?
(Average) (Skill 7.3)

A. Beginning

B. Intermediate

C. Advanced

D. Advanced high

Answer: A. Beginning
Juanita is unable to maintain conversations and relies on using words or phrases she has memorized. The other options are not correct as in each designation students understand and participate in conversations from simple to complex.

37. Mr. Martinez's use of positive feedback and relaxed discussion with Juanita best supports which of the following?
(Average) (Skill 6.4)

A. Cognitive processes toward reading comprehension

B. Creating a positive affective filter for Juanita

C. Increasing social abilities in speaking

D. Activating background knowledge to make cognitive connections

Answer: B. Creating a positive affective filter for Juanita
Mr. Martinez's dialogue supports Juanita's attitude toward participating in discussions and maintains her self-esteem by providing positive responses to her remarks. The affective domain is the feelings and emotions that a student has that affect how a second language is acquired. Option A is not correct as this discussion does not provide information that would support the use of cognitive processes. Option C is incorrect as this is not a social setting in which students are speaking. Option D is not correct because the discussion is not one in which Mr. Martinez is presenting questions that would support activating background knowledge of the student.

38. A high school English teacher is preparing a vocabulary lesson for her ESL class, based on a book that they will read. The best way for the teacher to introduce a word to students is to:
(Average) (Skill 5.1)

A. show students its dictionary definition and discuss its article of speech.

B. create a list of its synonyms and antonyms.

C. present the word in a variety of sentences and have students derive its meaning through context clues.

D. use the students' native language to define the word and use it in its context from the book.

Answer: C. present the word in a variety of sentences and have students derive its meaning through context clues
Option C is the best choice as students are involved in deriving the meaning of the word through its context in the sentence. Option A is incorrect; showing students its definition does not actively engage them in the discovery of the word nor is it a given that students will understand all the words in the definition. Option B is not correct as it is not a strategy by which students will internalize the meaning of the word. Option D is incorrect as the translation of the word in its context in the story may not translate true to its meaning in English.

39. Which of the following would be an appropriate writing task for beginning ELLs?
(Average) (Skill 5.2)

A. Reading the school menu and marking the ELL's choices

B. Taking notes on the daily activities into a class notebook

C. Copying a note inviting parents to a school meeting

D. Writing a letter to the editor of the school newspaper

Answer: C. Copying a note inviting parents to a school meeting
Tasks are loosely defined as activities that emphasize meaning over form. Option C is a writing task and the best choice. Option D is probably beyond the scope of beginning ELLs. Option A is a reading activity and not a writing task. Option B is a listening activity followed by a writing task.

40. **Ms. Ray is working with a second grade student who is considered a beginning ELL. She has letters on the table that spell the word** *cat.* **She has the student sound out the word by saying the sound of each letter. Ms. Ray then has the student read the word. She repeats this with the words** *hat* **and** *mat.* **Ms. Ray is developing the student's ability to do which of the following?**
(Rigorous) (Skill 5.3)

A. Repeated readings of high-frequency words

B. Sight word reading practice

C. Phoneme-grapheme correspondence

D. Reading of phonetically irregular words

Answer: C. Phoneme-grapheme correspondence
Ms. Ray is having the child say each letter sound before reading the word. She is teaching her student the relationship between the sound (phoneme) and the written symbol for that sound (grapheme). Option A is incorrect as the student is not repeatedly reading the word. Options B and D are not correct as these are neither sight words nor phonetically irregular words.

41. **Which one of the following is a way to help a student remember information?**
(Average) (Skill 5.4)

A. Establishing the purpose of the experiment

B. Recording information

C. Studying headings and subheadings

D. Creating artwork

Answer: D. Creating artwork
Establishing the purpose of the experiment is a prereading activity. Options B and C are reading activities. Option D is a postreading activity to help a student organize and remember information.

42. Ms. Ochoa is planning the vocabulary introduction to the new unit on Space in her middle school ELL science class. During her planning, she has created the following steps to follow for student understanding of the unit vocabulary:

- Teacher gives a description, explanation, or example for each word.
- Students restate or explain each word's meaning in their own words.
- Students create a picture or graphic for each word.
- Students discuss the terms with one another.

However, Ms. Ochoa felt that another step needed to be added in order to help ELLs create connections with prior knowledge of the terms being learned in this unit. Ms. Ochoa could:
(Rigorous) (Skill 5.5)

A. involve students in games that allow them to play with the vocabulary for this unit.

B. have students write the vocabulary and terms in a journal, including definitions and use in a sentence.

C. provide students with numerous print and media materials on the subject that re-enforce vocabulary and terms.

D. encourage students to create a content map in their native language (that also incorporates English terms) showing what they already know.

Answer: D. encourage students to create a content map in their native language (that also incorporates English terms) showing what they already know
Ms. Ochoa's goal is to have students make connections between what they know and what they are learning, transferring their knowledge from their first language to their second language. Encouraging students to create a content map, a form of graphic organizer, in their original language, will enable students to make connections to what they are learning. Option A does not take the students' native language into account, which is Ms. Ochoa's goal. Options B and C do not encourage the use of a student's native language.

43. An English teacher included a unit on fairy tales in her classroom. To promote critical literacy, she could have her students:
(Average) (Skill 5.6)

A. provide a list of prereading questions for discussion.

B. use a flowchart to outline the different plots.

C. compare the stories with their native-language versions.

D. make cartoon drawings illustrating the stories.

Answer: C. compare the stories to the native-language versions
Option A would activate previous knowledge and create interest in the tales. Option B suggests a flowchart could be used as a plot summary. Option D provides extra input for better understanding of the story and an artistic outlet for talented students. Only Option C gives students opportunities for critical analysis and a means of exploring universal themes in fairy tales around the world.

44. Mr. Hardy teaches a fourth grade ESL class. Knowing that his students come from a variety of backgrounds and development levels, he creates a game in which teams of students work at identifying common, everyday signs and text, such as menus, road signs, and so on. He expects students to respond in English, supporting each other in their teams. Based on this activity, Mr. Hardy is helping his ELL students to develop which skill?
(Rigorous)(Skill 5.6)

A. Association with everyday written items

B. Basic literacy skill of writing

C. A unified understanding of language

D. Connections between everyday items

Answer: A. Association with everyday written items
Mr. Hardy is helping students at various developmental levels make connections, or associations, to everyday items that they are familiar with. Option B is not correct as this activity does not address basic literacy skills in writing, but rather addresses a student's visual literacy. Option C is inappropriate because these students have a variety of backgrounds and development levels. Option D is incorrect because students are making connections not between items but rather to what they know about the items.

45. **Which one of the following has an impact on the literacy of an L2 student?**
(Rigorous) (Skill 5.7)

A. Familial literacy

B. Parents who read to their child

C. Parents involved in the child's schooling

D. All of the above

Answer: D. All of the above
Literacy development is affected not only by students' educational background, but also by the background and involvement of their families.

46. **Which one of the following is a CALP?**
(Rigorous) (Skill 6.1)

A. Review Chapter 1 for tomorrow's test.

B. Good morning.

C. Nice to meet you.

D. All of the above

Answer: A. Review Chapter 1 for tomorrow's test
Option A is a CALP or Cognitive Academic Language Proficiency skill. Options B and C are BICS or Basic Interpersonal Conversational Skills.

47. **Keeping a learning log is an example of which of the following integrated approaches to language teaching?**
(Easy) (Skill 6.2)

A. Graphic organizer

B. Task-based or experiential learning

C. Cooperative learning

D. Whole-language approach

Answer: D. Whole-language approach
The whole-language approach emphasizes an integrated language and content instructional approach. Some of the strategies include dialogue journals, reading response journals, learning logs, process-based writing, and language experience stories.

48. Which one of the following is NOT an advantage of learning and using more than one language?
(Average) (Skill 6.3)

A. Cognitive rigidity

B. Increased visual-social abilities

C. More logical reasoning skills

D. Better problem-solving and analytical skills

Answer: A. Cognitive rigidity
Options B, C, and D are all advantages of learning and using more than one language. Option A is the opposite of cognitive flexibility, another advantage of learning more than one language.

49. Which one of the following is NOT an instance of instrumental motivation in language learning?
(Rigorous) (Skill 6.4)

A. Moving to a different country or into another culture

B. Getting a job that requires speaking in a different language

C. Parents enrolling their child in a foreign language class

D. Desiring to communicate with other peoples and learn about their culture

Answer: D. Desiring to communicate with other peoples and learn about their culture
Options A, B, and C are all examples of instrumental motivation, in which the learner learns the language for a

specific reason. The circumstances of instrumental motivation are often beyond the control of the learner. Option D is an intrinsic desire on the part of a learner and an example of integrative motivation.

50. Which of the following is NOT an attribute of a viable test for ELLs?
(Average) (Skill 7.1)

A. Reliable

B. Valid

C. Cost-effective

D. Practical

Answer: C. Cost-effective
Reliability, validity, and practicality are the three attributes of a viable assessment test. A reliable test produces similar results when scored a second time. A valid test measures what it claims to measure. A practical test is easy to administer and easy to score. Option B is the correct response because, although cost-effectiveness may be a type of practicality, the other factors are more important to consider.

51. A middle school language arts teacher has a group of ELLs who have varying degrees of English-language abilities. While planning how to assess students' progress she relies on which of the following?
(Rigorous) (Skill 7.2)

A. Test scores that reflect the whole school population

B. The use of a bell curve to plot students' results and progress

C. Assessment results only in the areas of English in which they have achieved mastery

D. Observations, test scores, and samples of daily work

Answer: D. Observations, test scores, and samples of daily work
By using observations, test scores, and samples of daily work, the teacher will be able to assess each student's abilities in all four domains. Option A is incorrect as test scores of the whole school population do not provide a comprehensive evaluation of each individual ELL. Option B would not give an accurate result of individual abilities and progress. Option C would not produce a comprehensive evaluation.

52. Before the 2013–14 school year began, Ms. Rawlins took the time to look at the test scores of her incoming ELL Spanish-speaking sixth grade students. She noted that several of her ELLs took a modified STAAR test due to their language, but not because of a learning disability. Which of the following tests would they have taken?
(Easy) (Skill 7.3)

A. STAAR L

B. STAAR Modified

C. STAAR Spanish

D. STAAR Alternate

Answer: A. STAAR L
The STAAR L test is for ELLs who were first enrolled in grades 3 through 9 in 2011–12. Option B is not correct as this test is for those ELLs who were admitted in 2011–12 and who are receiving special education services with a disability. Option C is reserved for ELLs in grades 3 through 5. Option D is for all students in grades 3 through 8 who receive special education services and have a significant cognitive disability.

53. **An ESL teacher at a local middle school had to determine if an ELL needed to be retained. Which of the following standardized assessments should the teacher NOT take into consideration when making this decision?**
(Rigorous) (Skills 7.3, 7.5)

A. TELPAS

B. Previous TAKS scores (implemented before STAAR)

C. STAAR

D. All of the above

Answer: A. TELPAS
The TELPAS should not be taken into consideration as that test measures a student's progress within the content, not mastery of it. The TELPAS provides a continuous body of data of a student's acquisition of the English language. Options B and C could be used to determine if the student has mastered content or should be retained.

54. **According to the definition of LEPs in Title VII, which one of the following statements about LEPs is NOT applicable?**
(Average) (Skill 7.4)

A. The student is a native American or Alaska native.

B. The student not born in the United States.

C. The student is migratory.

D. The student gas little difficulty with English.

Answer: D. The student has little difficulty with English
Options A, B, and C are all included in the definition of Limited English Proficient students (LEPs) under Title VII.

55. **Before the school year began, Ms. Davilla decided to look through her fifth grade ELL records from the previous year. She wanted to know how her students performed on the final writing exam. In reviewing their scores, Ms. Davilla should look at which of the following to fully understand what skills her students mastered?**
(Rigorous) (Skill 7.5)

A. The final, overall writing score

B. The individually mastered TEKS

C. What modifications were used

D. The prompt that was given for the writing assignment

Answer: B. The individually mastered TEKS
Understanding what individual TEKS a student has mastered will give Ms. Davilla the most comprehensive look at each student. Options A, C, and D are incorrect because the overall score, modifications, nor the prompt will help Ms. Davilla understand what skills her ESL students did or did not master.

56. Which one of the following is a way that teachers can NOT use the information gathered in testing?
(Rigorous) (Skill 7.6)

A. To improve their teaching

B. To demonstrate a special needs student's deficiencies

C. To orient their teaching practices in more desirable ways

D. To plan remedial work

Answer: B. To demonstrate a special needs student's deficiencies
Options A, C, and D are all ways information gathered from testing serves teachers and their students. Option B is only the first step in identifying a special needs student and is only preliminary diagnostic information. Many ELLs are incorrectly labeled as special needs, and great care must be used to determine if the language deficiencies are ELL problems or special needs problems.

57. Which of the following is NOT a requirement for schools to meet based on the Lau Plan (*Lau* v. *Nichols*)?
(Average) (Skill 8.1)

A. Provide all students with the same textbooks, teachers, and curriculums

B. Identify assessments and evaluative tools for ongoing assessment

C. Form and convene a Language Proficiency Assessment Committee (LPAC)

D. Outline specific staff responsibilities and credentials for instruction

Answer: A. Provide all students with the same textbooks, teachers, and curriculums
Schools must now follow the Supreme Court ruling that recognizes that not all students will understand English, and therefore they would be excluded from a meaningful education due to lack of language skills in reading, writing, listening, and speaking. Therefore, schools must use materials that support students' learning of the second language. Options B, C, and D are requirements for schools based on the *Lau* v. *Nichols* (1974) ruling.

58. The No Child Left Behind (NCLB) Act does NOT require schools to:
(Rigorous) (Skill 8.1)

A. give assessment in English if the LEP has received three years of schooling in the U.S. (except for Puerto Rico).

B. measure school districts by status.

C. inform parents of the school's evaluation.

D. increase the length of the school year.

Answer: D. increase the length of the school year
Options A, B, and C are all requirements of the NCLB Act. Option D is of concern to many educators who feel that the length of the school day and the number of days in the year students attend school is far below that of other industrialized countries and should be increased.

59. Which one of the following methods aims for English proficiency?
(Rigorous) (Skill 8.2)

A. Canadian French Immersion Program

B. Indigenous language immersion programs

C. Structured English immersion

D. Submersion with primary language support

Answer: C. Structured English immersion
The goal of the methods in options A, B, and D is bilingualism; ELLs are given sheltered instruction. In Option C, structured English immersion, the goal is to achieve English proficiency.

60. At a local elementary school, there has been a large influx of bilingual and ESL Spanish-speaking students in the primary grades. Based on the sudden change in population, the school's administration needs to make management decisions on available resources based on which of the following?
(Average) (Skill 8.3)

A. District demographics

B. Student characteristics

C. District resources

D. School resources

Answer: D. School resources
The school is experiencing the influx and will have to adjust its infrastructure and reallocate personnel resources to ensure that students' needs are met. Options A and C are not correct because this is not a shift in a district's overall demographics. Option B is incorrect because the characteristics of the students will be similar in language needs while academic needs will be taken into consideration after the school reallocates personnel and resources.

61. Which of the following instructional approaches emphasizes LEPs' acquiring new language skills through the content areas?
(Average) (Skills 5.6, 8.4)

A. TPR

B. Natural Approach

C. CALLA

D. Communicative Approach

Answer: C. CALLA
CALLA (Cognitive Academic Language Learning Approach) was developed by Chamot and O'Malley. CALLA integrates language development, content-area instruction, and explicit instruction in learning strategies.

62. Ms. Wilson asked her students to act as translators during recent family conferences. In one instance, the father looked increasingly anxious as he struggled to make himself understood. What went wrong?
(Average) (Skill 9.1)

A. The father was insulted by the situation.

B. The ELL was a good student and translated the teacher's comments well.

C. The ELL was reluctant to translate.

D. The father was proud of his son's/daughter's skill.

Answer: A. The father was insulted by the situation
Option A is the most likely cause of the tension. The teacher demonstrated poor cultural awareness of the situation though her intentions were good. Asking children to translate in parent-student conferences is a poor strategy since it upsets the hierarchy of authority in most families by ignoring the authority of the parents.

63. Mr. Sanchez, a new ESOL instructor, wanted to establish a highly effective learning classroom for his students. Which of the following would be conducive to his goal?
(Average) (Skill 9.2)

A. Lots of educational technology

B. A large classroom library

C. Textbooks of different reading levels

D. All of the above

Answer: D. All of the above
To create a classroom that is highly effective for ELLs, the environment needs to be language-enriched, which is the key to comprehensible input and high motivation.

64. Which one of the following actions will help an ELL adjust to a new school and provide a positive learning environment?
(Average) (Skill 9.3)

A. Placing the ELL in a group of all English speakers

B. Calling on the newcomer frequently to make him/her feel like part of the class

C. Assigning a classmate to guide him/her through essential routines

D. Urging the newcomer to tell the class about his/her homeland

Answer: C. Assigning a classmate to guide him/her through essential routines
Most newcomers want to fit in without drawing attention to themselves. Especially if they have come from situations in which their lives were in turmoil (such as a war zone or where they were persecuted for their race or beliefs), they need to learn the classroom routines and procedures in a tranquil fashion and join discussions as they feel capable. Encouragement is good, but it should be without heavy-handed pressure. Option C is the correct response since having a peer to guide him/her will reduce much of the ELL's anxiety in adjusting to a stressful new environment.

65. Which of the following is a reason to offer classroom lectures instead of cooperative group work?
(Easy) (Skill 9.4)

A. They increase student concentration.

B. Students learn better.

C. The teacher is seen as an academic authority.

D. Group work is unproductive.

Answer: C. The teacher is seen as an academic authority.
Teaching ELLs is a rewarding yet challenging profession. Often our own beliefs are challenged by the cultural beliefs of others. Option D can be discarded since the statement is false. Options A and B may be true for some students. The best choice is Option C, since in some cultures the teacher is seen as an academic authority, and until the students learn the value of group work, it may be necessary to reinforce learning with teacher lectures.

66. A teacher who decides that her ELLs are lazy and indifferent to learning about U.S. culture is guilty of which of the following? *(Rigorous) (Skills 9.3, 9.5)*

A. Racism

B. Stereotyping

C. Discrimination

D. Ethnocentrism

Answer: B. Stereotyping
Stereotyping is attributing false or exaggerated characteristics of a group to an individual. Racism is discrimination based on race. Discrimination is negative behavior or treatment that a person shows when he or she is prejudiced against another person or group. Ethnocentrism is the belief in the superiority of one culture over another, such as U.S. culture being superior.

67. At the beginning of the school year, the ESL teacher provided parents with information on the services offered at the local library in their native language. The information covered online resources, free language classes, and after-school tutoring. It is obvious that the ESL teacher understands the importance of which of the following? *(Rigorous) (Skill 10.1)*

A. Collaborating effectively with parents and guardians of ELL students

B. Communicating general information about English and English-language instruction

C. Facilitating participation in school activities

D. Advocating educational and social equity for ELLs

Answer: D. Advocating educational and social equity for ELLs
The teacher is advocating educational and social equity for ELLs by providing information in the native language about resources that are available to everyone. Option A is incorrect because providing information is not collaborating. Option B is not correct because the teacher is providing information on resources that include English-language instruction. Option C is not correct as information was not given about school activities.

68. **The majority of ELLs in Mr. Sosa's ESL class lack basic technology in the home. Wanting to develop computer literacy in his students, Mr. Sosa implements an evening class in the computer lab for students and their family members on using the Internet and district databases as a means of supporting classroom lessons. Mr. Sosa also sets aside a time once a week during the day for parents to come in and use the computer lab to access their children's online records and classwork. Based on this information, it is obvious that Mr. Sosa understands:**
(Rigorous) (Skill 10.2)

A. the importance of family involvement in their child's learning.

B. that advocating for ELLs will ensure their participation in learning.

C. that it is important to communicate and collaborate with school personnel about the use of school resources.

D. the importance of encouraging constructive use of students' time while at school.

Answer: A. the importance of family involvement in their child's learning
Mr. Sosa realizes the importance of family participation in students' learning, and he has created a means whereby families can participate to develop computer literacy. Option B is not correct as this is not a situation that requires an advocacy approach to solve the need. Option C is not correct as there is no evidence of collaboration with school personnel in this scenario. Option D is incorrect as this does not reflect Mr. Sosa's goal of involving family members in their children's learning.

69. **Which one of the following is the best reason for encouraging outreach programs in which family members are involved in school activities?**
(Average) (Skill 10.3)

A. The program provides extra support for students.

B. Parents can provide discipline for their children.

C. Parents learn life skills for the new country.

D. It's easier to ask for additional resources directly from parents.

Answer: A. The program provides extra support for students
When schools and parents have a close relationship, students receive the benefit of an additional support system. Option A is the best answer.

70. Which one of the following points is the most important reason for inviting speakers from the ELLs' community to the classroom? *(Average) (Skill 10.4)*

A. Increasing students' knowledge

B. Motivating ELLs to succeed

C. Advocating for increased funding

D. Encouraging good student behavior

Answer: B. Motivating ELLs to succeed
The main reason for inviting guest speakers from the community and the students' language groups is to motivate them to succeed just as the guest has. Option A is just one reason for inviting guest speakers. Options C and D can be dismissed as invalid reasons for inviting guest speakers.

1. **Phonetic languages are those in which:**
   (Average) (Skill 1.1)

   A. there is a one-to-one correspondence between letters and sounds.

   B. phonemes are the smallest unit of sound.

   C. consonants are phonemes.

   D. alliterative words result in different meanings.

DIRECTIONS: Use the information below to answer the questions that follow.

Ms. Ailara's seventh-grade ELLs are assigned a partner and each pair of students has a script of dialogue that they will follow. Below is part of an example of one of the scripts.

Student 1: *Hello. My name is _____. What is your name?*

Student 2: *Hello. My name is _____. How are you today?*

Student 1: *I am fine. How are you?*

Student 2: *I am fine. Thank you. What have you been doing?*

After discussing the experience with her students, Ms. Ailara shows a short video where two students meet and greet each other at a party in a more informal manner, using slang and abbreviated word forms. The class discusses the difference between what they have seen and what they experienced in their earlier activity.

2. **By using scripted dialogue, the teacher demonstrates that she knows the importance of which of the following?**
   (Rigorous) (Skill 1.1)

   A. Having two students speak together–one experienced in English while the other is not

   B. Teaching students how to speak in complete sentences

   C. Using set dialogues to help students learn the patterns of English discourse

   D. Developing students' comfort level with each other

3. **The video of the students greeting each other at a party is an example of which type of language usage?**
   (Average) (Skill 1.2)

   A. Standard American English usage

   B. Formal language register

   C. Academic discourse

   D. Social register

4. **Based on Ms. Ailara's activity with her students and the viewed video, it is obvious that Ms. Ailara realizes that the affective, linguistic, and cognitive needs of ESL students should be experienced in what way?** *(Rigorous) (Skill 9.2)*

   A. Through guided discussions and open-ended questions

   B. Studied in context with examples of real-world applications

   C. Within age-appropriate academic scenarios

   D. Through carefully planned curriculum expectations

5. **Which one of the following is an example of code switching?** *(Average) (Skill 1.2)*

   A. Making gestures

   B. Calling a school "la escuela" when speaking English

   C. Using jargon, for example, "apps"

   D. Simplifying language for ELLs

6. **Which of the following researchers emphasized the importance of focusing on all four communicative language skills at the same time?** *(Average) (Skill 1.3)*

   A. Genesee

   B. Nunan

   C. Cummins

   D. Krashen

7. **A high school ESL teacher introduces the following words and phrases before having a class discussion on their writing assignment for the day: "help," "don't do that," "no," "please help." These expressions represent which part of speech?** *(Easy) (Skill 1.4)*

   A. Conjunction

   B. Preposition

   C. Verb

   D. Interjection

8. **Which one of the following is the single most important factor affecting language acquisition?** *(Rigorous) (Skill 2.1)*

   A. Onset of puberty

   B. Baby-talk (proto-conversations)

   C. Self-confidence

   D. Comprehensible input

DIRECTIONS: Use the information below to answer the questions that follow.

Ms. Mendoza's kindergarten ESL class is a busy place. A classroom observer notes that Ms. Mendoza's students are paired up or work in groups in a problem-solving, discovery format to learn basic numerical concepts. Students are on task in the centers, speaking in both their native language and in English as they interact, often intermingling both languages into sentences. In reviewing Ms. Mendoza's student data, it is obvious that there has been a continual improvement in students' mathematical understanding.

9. **It is clear from the description of the students' behavior that Ms. Mendoza:**
    (Rigorous) (Skill 2.2)

    A. knows how to implement the district's requirement for developing cognitive growth.

    B. uses theories and research to provide the appropriate strategies for language and concept acquisition.

    C. knows how to meet the needs of individual ELLs.

    D. knows how to create a classroom structure for input and output of information.

10. **Ms. Mendoza allows students to intermingle both languages while working in centers because she realizes that:**
    (Rigorous) (Skill 2.4)

    A. language is acquired lineally and not influenced by individual factors.

    B. students need structured activities that allow them to follow their own interests in their own time frame in a supportive environment.

    C. interlanguage is a strategy used by second-language learners to compensate for lack of proficiency in the new language.

    D. students need to cooperate with others, interacting and working with a native speaker of the language being learned.

DIRECTIONS: Use the information below to answer the questions that follow.

During a classroom conversation in a high school self-contained English class the following was overheard by the lead ELL teacher for the school.

Instructor: *Now who can tell me about the character's actions in the second chapter? Olette?*

Olette: *She is embarrassed.*

Instructor: *No, I want to know about the character's actions in the second chapter. Olette, can you try again?*

Olette: [struggling and not looking the instructor in the eye] *She act embarrassed.*

Instructor: *No, you still aren't telling me about the character's actions. Try again, Olette.*

Olette refuses to answer and scoots down in her seat and pretends to study the text. The instructor moves on to other students.

11. **Based on the scenario, it is obvious that the instructor does not understand or is not aware of which of the following strategies?** *(Average) (Skill 2.3)*

    A. Cognitive

    B. Metacognitive

    C. Social

    D. Socioaffective

12. **The lead ELL teacher meets with the instructor and they discuss the various strategies that could have been used to bolster Olette's affective learning level. Which of the following would have been the best strategies the instructor could have used in this situation?** *(Rigorous) (Skill 2.3)*

    A. Positive acknowledgment; clarifying expectations for the answer

    B. Giving the correct answer to the question

    C. Asking another student to answer for Olette and explain why the answer was correct

    D. Repeat the question slowly and with correct enunciation of each word

13. **Which one of the following is a metacognitive strategy for ELLs?** *(Rigorous) (Skill 2.3)*

    A. Setting reasonable goals

    B. Constant repetition

    C. Concentration on sounds

    D. Risk taking

14. Which of the following is the correct explanation of the PPP model?
(Easy) (Skill 2.5)

A. Practice, Production, and Proficiency

B. Practice, Presentation, and Production

C. Presentation, Practice, and Production

D. Production, Practice, and Presentation

15. Which one of the following statements is NOT true about instructional design?
(Average) (Skill 3.1)

A. ELLs need many opportunities to work with different people during collaborative activities.

B. ELLs' interest is maintained by combining students' interests and curriculum objectives.

C. The classroom atmosphere should be supportive.

D. Learning activities are organized to repeat the same instructional point until it is mastered.

DIRECTIONS: Use the information below to answer the questions that follow.

Ms. Nguyen, a second grade teacher, has developed a word-study activity for her class of English-speaking students and ELLs. The activity is a review from the week's lessons on complete, simple sentences. In this activity, students work with a partner to create complete, simple sentences using preselected sight words from the Dolch word list. After a brief review and modeling what constitutes a simple sentence, Ms. Nguyen gives each pair of students a set of word cards as follows:

| I | go | me | home | and | with |

| to | the | to | school | brother | like |

Ms. Nguyen also gives them the following directions:

1. Working with your partner, make a sentence using these words.
2. Use as many words as possible.
3. You may not add other words.
4. Write the sentence in your journals.

16. While observing her students, Ms. Nguyen realizes that another step added to the instructions would better support the learning of the ELLs in this activity. Which of the following would be the best addition to support the ELLs?
(Average) (Skill 3.2)

A. The first word needs to be capitalized, and the sentence should end with a period.

B. Read the sentence aloud to your partner. Does it make sense?

C. You may add other words to your sentence.

D. You must use all the words.

17. On reviewing anecdotal records and finished products during this activity, Ms. Nguyen found that many of her beginning and intermediate ELLs struggled with the activity while her advanced ELL and English-speaking students were successful. Which of the following should best be considered by Ms. Nguyen for future activities?
(Rigorous) (Skills 4.2, 4.6)

A. The difficulty level of sight words used for sentence-building activities

B. The importance of reviewing the basic structure of academic expectations, as in this case, a complete, simple sentence

C. The inclusion of native-language materials during an activity

D. The academic strengths of each student when assigning partners

18. To accommodate beginning ELLs in the class, the most appropriate strategy Ms. Nguyen should implement for this activity is to:
(Rigorous) (Skill 6.2)

A. include sight words that are more challenging.

B. model and preteach the activity before beginning it.

C. include illustrations on the appropriate word cards.

D. allow those students to observe and not participate if they choose not to.

DIRECTIONS: Use the information below to answer the questions that follow.

Mr. Roma is presenting a new unit on insects to his fifth grade ESL science class. Based on previous lessons, he knows that his class has little knowledge of the natural world. A small portion of the discussion is given below.

Mr. Roma: *Insects are not mammals, nor birds. Rather, insects are a unique species of which there are more than 800,000 types. Some insects you may know are ladybugs, grasshoppers, beetles, and ants. There are many identifying characteristics of insects. All insects have three pairs of legs and three body parts. Now that I've given you this overview, I want each of you to read pages 45 through 69 in your science book in your groups. Are there any questions? Yes, Emmanuel?*

Emmanuel: *Um, Mr. Roma. I do not understand what insects are?*

Mr. Roma: *Insects.* [He writes the word on the board.] *There are more than 800,000 types of insects, or what you might call bugs. There are ladybugs, grasshoppers, beetles, and ants.* [He writes the words on the board.] *But there are so many more insects! All insects have certain characteristics, or ways, to identify them. Insects have three body parts. All insects have six legs, which are three pairs of legs. We have one pair of legs, and an insect has 3 pairs of legs. Having 3 body parts and 3 pairs of legs is a characteristic of insects.* [He writes this information on the board.]

19. **Mr. Roma understands the support that is needed for his ESL students during classroom presentations and discussions. Based on this portion of the presentation it is obvious that Mr. Roma realizes the importance of:** *(Rigorous) (Skill 4.2)*

    A. carefully listening to his students and their questions.

    B. summarizing the information that he gives to his students.

    C. paraphrasing the information that he presents to his students.

    D. turn-taking during the conversation as he presents information.

20. **Based on this scenario, what is an additional resource that Mr. Roma should have provided to help his students make connections to what he was saying?**
(Rigorous) (Skill 3.2)

   A. Brainstorming opportunities to generate ideas as to what an insect is

   B. A list of vocabulary words that would be used during the lesson

   C. A copy of his discussion and notes

   D. Visual supports, such as photos, charts, and diagrams

21. **Mr. Roma wants to support his students in learning the information about insects so they can compare insects to spiders during the next day's lesson. Which of the following would NOT help his students understand and organize information so that comparisons could be made between insects and spiders?**
(Rigorous) (Skill 3.2)

   A. After the presentation and reading the selection in groups, students web out the information learned.

   B. In groups, students will create concept maps about the subject being studied.

   C. A variety of scaffolded texts on the subject is provided to help students identify facts and details.

   D. Each student uses numerous texts on spiders and insects.

22. **Mr. Roma decides to have his students create semantic maps of the vocabulary that they are learning during this study. Which of the following skills will his ELLs develop by doing that?**
(Rigorous) (Skill 6.2)

   A. The ability to organize and categorize information gathered

   B. The ability to make comparisons and recognize similarities between two items

   C. Prioritization of the information that is gathered during the activity

   D. Recognition of the sequence of the information gathered

23. **Which one of the following is a scaffolding technique?**
(Easy) (Skill 3.3)

   A. A pretest

   B. Individual projects

   C. Playing games

   D. Using rubrics

24. In order for an ELL to fully benefit from using the Internet on a topic or concept, which of the following should be observed? *(Easy) (Skill 3.4)*

   A. Topics should have specific goals and be timely

   B. Teachers must be computer specialists

   C. Communication is not required between teacher and student

   D. Results do not have to be shared

25. Which one of the following is NOT an effective classroom management technique? *(Average) (Skill 3.5)*

   A. Implementing techniques that focus on the positive

   B. Anticipating possible problems

   C. Teaching the expected behaviors early in the school year

   D. Deciding on inappropriate behaviors as they occur

26. Ms. Chan has made an anchor chart for her ELL middle school language arts class. The chart contains a variety of sentence stems for students to use when responding to questions in the text they are reading. For example, ____ *is similar to* ___ *because both are* ____ . After reviewing the sentence stems with students, Ms. Chan's class is more participatory during the class discussion. Ms. Chan's activity is promoting which of the following? *(Rigorous) (Skill 4.1)*

   A. Listening to the information being given

   B. Encouraging oral responses

   C. Providing support in writing responses

   D. Improving the students' reading abilities

27. Which one of the following techniques shows how questioning should NOT be used when teaching interpersonal communication skills? *(Average) (Skill 4.2)*

   A. Encouraging dialogue

   B. Checking for comprehension

   C. Requiring a one- or two-word answer in initial stages

   D. Interrogating

28. Which one of the following is a valid ELL instructional method for communicating with students? *(Easy) (Skill 4.3)*

A. Rapid-fire commands

B. Gestures

C. Speaking normally

D. Introducing new vocabulary in sentences

29. Ms. Misra's ESL seventh grade biology class has been studying a variety of mammals and their body systems. During the course of their studies, students created concept maps of vocabulary and illustrations of key points for individual presentations. Before presenting their information to the class, Ms. Misra has students pair up and share their information with each other. What is the purpose of this interaction? *(Rigorous) (Skill 4.4)*

A. To check for correctness of information

B. To prepare for a class assessment

C. Oral rehearsal of learning

D. Management of content information

30. Which of the following differences in the English language would cause difficulties for a speaker of French? *(Rigorous) (Skill 4.5)*

A. The alphabetic writing system

B. Multiple vowel sounds represented in spelling

C. Rhetorical questions

D. Reading from left to right

31. Which of the following options is a nonintrusive way to give corrective feedback on written work? *(Average) (Skill 4.7)*

A. Writing an evaluative comment

B. Commenting on how to improve the assignment

C. Asking the ELL to redo the assignment

D. Thumbs up

32. Which one of the following is the least effective method of teaching vocabulary to older ELLs? *(Rigorous) (Skill 5.1)*

A. Using vocabulary words in a writing activity

B. Activating prior knowledge

C. Explicit strategy instruction

D. Studying vocabulary lists

33. For the ELL to achieve fluency in both speaking and reading, the least effective activity for ELLs is probably:
(Easy) (Skill 5.2)

A. ample speaking activities.

B. playing computer games.

C. reading widely.

D. singing songs.

34. While analyzing the reading assessment scores of her third grade ELLs, Ms. San Miguel noticed that the ELLs' fluency scores were low. Knowing the importance of fluency, which of the following strategies would benefit her students' fluency development?
(Rigorous) (Skill 5.3)

A. Modeled and repeated reading of familiar texts

B. Guided discussions through open-ended questions about the text

C. Skimming and scanning for specific information before reading

D. Restating information just read

35. Which of the following terms explains "it" in the sentence, "Although the aircraft had been damaged, it could still fly"?
(Rigorous) (Skill 5.4)

A. Chunking

B. Anaphoric reference

C. Cohesive device

D. Idiomatic expression

36. Which one of the following statements about prior knowledge is false?
(Easy) (Skill 5.5)

A. Prior knowledge helps learners to understand and to remember more.

B. Prior knowledge must be activated to improve comprehension.

C. Failure to activate prior knowledge may cause poor readers.

D. Good readers may reject an author's premise if it conflicts with prior knowledge.

37. At the beginning of a new semester, Mr. Choe wants to have students in his fifth grade ESL science class introduce themselves to their classmates. Which of the following would be the best activity for students to present to accomplish this?
(Rigorous) (Skill 5.6)

A. An oral PowerPoint presentation

B. An illustrated autobiographical poster

C. A written essay to be shared with the class

D. A show-and-tell presentation format with photos and illustrations

DIRECTIONS: Use the information below to answer the questions that follow.

Mr. Steiner, a language arts high school teacher, has a class of ESL students whose English-language abilities vary from beginning to advanced. Based on family language surveys, he notes that the majority of students are not exposed to English outside of the classroom.

38. What is the best purpose for having and referring to a family language survey?
(Rigorous) (Skill 5.7)

A. To decide what strategies to use to help students with their English acquisition

B. To determine if it would be better to begin instruction in students' native language To recognize and act on the personal factors that can affect students' English literacy development

C. To recognize and act on the personal factors that can affect students' English literacy development

D. To determine what level to begin students' instruction

39. Which of the following would best strengthen Mr. Steiner's understanding of his students' current second-language acquisition?
(Average) (Skill 7.3)

A. STAAR Spanish test results

B. TELPAS proficiency results

C. LPAC decisions

D. ELPS

DIRECTIONS: Use the information below to answer the questions that follow.

An ESL second grade teacher is teaming up with the school's Inclusion Strategist to introduce mammals to students by using technology, print materials, videos, and live examples. While preparing for the lessons, both teachers agree to help students connect to prior knowledge; they decide to begin the unit by using a graphic organizer (a concept map). In this graphic organizer, students list the four main characteristics of mammals. Then, during presentation and discussion, students fill in the organizer, discussing names of animals that they know match the information given.

40. This lesson is effective for ELLs because it helps them to develop which of the following?
(Average) (Skill 6.1)

A. Multiple perspectives of the language

B. Confidence in note taking

C. Making connections with background knowledge

D. English language attainment

41. **ELLs develop which of the following skills while creating their own graphic organizer or concept map?**
(Rigorous) (Skill 6.2)

A. Identifying main idea and supporting details

B. Making comparisons and recognizing similarities between items

C. Organizing and categorizing information

D. Listing information in sequential order

42. **Which one of the following is among the reasons to develop problem-solving skills in the second language?**
(Average) (Skill 6.3)

A. Enhances cognition in the first language

B. Reduces tension in the classroom

C. Increases spatial skills

D. Reduces intuition

43. **Which one of the following conditions might cause a previously motivated student to lose interest in school?**
(Easy) (Skill 6.4)

A. Peer or familial pressure

B. Anxiety about his or her performance

C. Ridicule from native English-speaking classmates

D. All of the above

44. **Which one of the following tests would be appropriate to screen candidates for a position as an international airport announcer?**
(Average) (Skill 7.1)

A. An achievement test

B. A diagnostic test

C. A proficiency test

D. A communicative language test

45. **Which one of the following is an example of alternative testing?**
(Average) (Skill 7.2)

A. Unit exams

B. TOEFL

C. Experiments and/or demonstrations

D. AAPPL

46. A tenth grade ELL who enrolled during the 2013–14 school year is currently receiving special education services and is found to have a disability that severely affects his academic progress. Based on this information, his teacher approaches the ARD committee and LPAC to verify the level of STAAR test that he will take. What would be the proper test to administer to this student? *(Rigorous) (Skill 7.3)*

A. STAAR Alternate

B. STAAR L

C. STAAR Modified

D. STAAR Spanish

47. Brittany, an ELL fifth grade student, passed the STAAR exam with commendations in reading, writing, and mathematics. She also maintained straight A averages in grades 3, 4, and 5. Based on this information, the LPAC decided to exit Brittany from the ESL program. Based on the LPAC decision, you can assume that Brittany scored which of the following on her TELPAS exam? *(Easy) (Skill 7.4)*

A. Beginning

B. Intermediate

C. Advanced

D. Advanced high

48. Which of the following assessments is used as an accurate measure of student achievement in reading, writing, mathematics, science, and social studies? *(Easy) (Skill 7.5)*

A. TAKS

B. AAPPL

C. TELPAS

D. STAAR

49. The purpose of assessment is: *(Average) (Skill 7.6)*

A. diagnostic and ongoing.

B. to judge a student's learning.

C. to compare student performance against grade-level standards.

D. All of the above

50. Which of the following legislative acts or Supreme Court rulings prohibits schools from excluding students from federal education programs? *(Rigorous) (Skill 8.1)*

A. Civil Rights Act of 1964

B. *Lau* v. *Nichols*

C. *Castaneda* v. *Pickard*

D. No Child Left Behind Act

51. Which of the following is NOT an ESL pull-out model?
(Average) (Skill 8.2)

A. Grammar-based

B. Communication-based

C. Self-contained

D. Content-based

52. Which of the following factors will have an influence on the decision of which type of ESL program is chosen for a school district?
(Average) (Skill 8.3)

A. School demographics

B. Nearby magnet school

C. Availability of resources

D. All of the above

DIRECTIONS: Use the information below to answer the questions that follow.

During Mr. Antoine's initial observations of his new middle school students, he overhears the following conversation between two girls.

Xochitl: *Hi! My name is Xochitl. We are sitting together in math. What's your name?*

Jasmin: *My name is Jasmin.*

Xochitl: *Are you excited about school?*

Jasmin: [shrugs] *English not good. I guess?*

Xochitl: *Want to meet my friends?*

Jasmin: *No, no. I not talk good. I need study.* [Jasmin walks away.]

Over the next several weeks, Mr. Antoine realizes that Jasmin does not interact with other students and will not participate in class discussions over topics and concepts. Knowing that this affects her oral-language development, he creates lessons and activities with instructional goals to increase Jasmin's oral-language proficiency among her peers.

53. Which of the following strategies should Mr. Antoine use to best help Jasmin at her current level of oral-language proficiency?
(Average) (Skill 8.4)

A. TPR

B. Dialogue journals

C. CALLA

D. Reciprocal teaching strategy

54. To best meet the instructional goals for Jasmin, Mr. Antoine should create lessons that include:
(Rigorous) (Skill 9.5)

A. the rules of polite conversation.

B. class discussions reviewing why each lesson is important.

C. silent, sustained reading.

D. small-group work that incorporates speaking activities.

55. Which one of the following instructional techniques is most appropriate for children during the "silent period" of language learning?
(Average) (Skill 8.4)

A. Computer games

B. TPR

C. Lectures

D. Drills

56. During class discussion in Ms. Baxter's eighth grade ESL American history class, Fong participated in the discussion but would not look Ms. Baxter in the face when responding to questions. In conferencing with Fong's other teachers, Ms. Baxter found that this was a common behavior in all his classes. Wanting Fong to participate more fully in class, Ms. Baxter would best take which course of action next?
(Rigorous) (Skill 9.1)

A. Speak with Fong to determine the reason for his evasive participation

B. Research Fong's cultural customs

C. Work with Fong one-on-one to develop classroom participation skills

D. Discuss with Fong expectations for participation in the academic classroom

57. Which one of the following is NOT a characteristic of culture affecting an ELL's language learning?
(Average) (Skill 9.1)

A. Reason for immigrating to the U.S.

B. Language

C. History

D. Arts

58. Which one of the following is NOT a valid reason for studying the history and art of an ELL's culture?
(Average) (Skill 9.1)

A. Helps students to broaden their knowledge base.

B. Encourages critical thinking.

C. Leads to greater understanding among people.

D. Disputes claims of superiority of the native culture.

59. **Which one of the following approaches ignores most Native American cultural beliefs?** *(Rigorous) (Skill 9.1)*

   A. Allow students to work as a team.

   B. Utilize learning in natural settings.

   C. Encourage the competitive spirit of the individual.

   D. Recognize the importance of silence.

60. **Which one of the following is NOT a task-based activity?** *(Average) (Skill 9.2)*

   A. Numbering a group of items in the correct order

   B. Labeling a map with the correct words

   C. Role plays

   D. Memorizing a list of spelling words

61. **Which one of the following would probably lead to language-minority parents participating in their children's education?** *(Average) (Skill 9.3)*

   A. Flyers sent home inviting parents to the school

   B. Cultural activities explaining U.S. holidays, for example, Thanksgiving

   C. Instructional materials for parents to use to support learning

   D. Administrators trained to service language minority groups

62. **Which of the following instructional techniques do NOT demonstrate cultural sensitivity?** *(Average) (Skill 9.4)*

   A. Using reading material of high literary quality

   B. Keeping a teaching log

   C. Using a wide variety of reading materials

   D. Urging slow-responding students to speak up

63. Which one of the following should be avoided when selecting reading materials for the classroom?
(Easy) (Skill 9.4)

A. Multicultured protagonists

B. Distorted gender roles

C. Settings in different countries

D. Different genres

64. Which of the following statements about culture and its manifestations is the most likely to cause learning difficulties for the ELL?
(Average) (Skills 9.4, 9.5)

A. Learning a language involves learning about the culture.

B. ELLs may not understand culture and its differences.

C. Teachers may offend students when they ignore cultural differences.

D. ELLs often believe their culture is superior to the one they are learning.

65. Which of the following activities is a valid advocacy for the ELL instructor to engage in?
(Average) (Skill 10.1)

A. Emphasizing culturally sensitive assessment

B. Eliminating reading programs dealing with stereotypes

C. Insisting on high-quality language arts programs for young children

D. All of the above

66. The lead ESL teacher at a local elementary school has been asked to present a district workshop for new hires on the comprehension needs of primary ELLs. Which of the following would be the best types of information for the ESL teacher to provide that meet the needs of a new primary ELL?
(Average) (Skill 10.1)

A. How to introduce students to correct pronunciation of basic English sight words followed by memorization techniques

B. A list of cultural taboos of the various nationalities that make up the district's ELL population

C. How best to check for comprehension in the ELL and the awareness and control of using certain parts of speech

D. A detailed analysis of the various nationalities, their native language structures, and how best to implement the ELPS

67. **Which of the following is a way to include all the community stakeholders in school activities?** *(Easy) (Skill 10.2)*

   A. Parent-teacher organizations

   B. Tutors

   C. Room parents

   D. All of the above

68. **The lead ESL teacher in a middle school's language arts program holds a monthly meeting with her ELLs' families to provide information and encourage participation in classroom projects. This practice shows that the teacher is aware of which of the following factors that affect language development?** *(Rigorous) (Skill 10.2)*

   A. Family involvement provides students with opportunities for academic communication.

   B. Families with positive experiences of school and learning are more likely to have children who develop English-language proficiency.

   C. The more information family members have about language instruction, the better able they are to teach their child the intricacies of the language.

   D. Through these meetings, ELLs' family members are better able to determine the effectiveness of the ESL program.

69. **Which one of the following is a valid way to communicate data about students?** *(Easy) (Skill 10.3)*

   A. Parent-teacher conferences

   B. Phone calls to parents

   C. Newsletters sent home

   D. All of the above

70. **The act before the U.S. Congress that would bring legalization to thousands of alien minors is called which of the following?** *(Easy) (Skill 10.4)*

   A. Illegal Aliens Act (IAA)

   B. Alien Minorities Protection Act (AMPA)

   C. Development, Relief, and Education of Alien Minors (DREAM) Act

   D. Safe Harbor Act for Minor's Education (SHAME)

SAMPLE TEST 2 ANSWER KEY AND RIGOR TABLE

Sample Test 2 Answer Key

1. A	11. D	21. D	31. B	41. C	51. C	61. D
2. C	12. A	22. A	32. D	42. A	52. D	62. D
3. D	13. A	23. D	33. B	43. D	53. C	63. B
4. B	14. C	24. A	34. A	44. C	54. D	64. C
5. B	15. D	25. D	35. B	45. C	55. B	65. D
6. A	16. C	26. B	36. C	46. C	56. B	66. C
7. D	17. D	27. D	37. B	47. D	57. A	67. D
8. A	18. C	28. B	38. C	48. D	58. D	68. B
9. B	19. C	29. C	39. B	49. A	59. C	69. D
10. C	20. D	30. B	40. C	50. A	60. D	70. C

Sample Test 2 Rigor Table

Rigor Level	Questions
Easy (20%)	7, 14, 23, 24, 28, 33, 36, 43, 47, 48, 63, 67, 69, 70
Average (40%)	1, 3, 5, 6, 11, 15, 16, 25, 27, 31, 39, 40, 42, 44, 45, 49, 51, 52, 53, 55, 57, 58, 60, 61, 62, 64, 65, 66
Rigorous (40%)	2, 4, 8, 9, 10, 12, 13, 17, 18, 19, 20, 21, 22, 26, 29, 30, 32, 34, 35, 37, 38, 41, 46, 50, 54, 56, 59, 68

SAMPLE TEST 2 ANSWERS WITH RATIONALES

1. **Phonetic languages are those in which:**
   (Average) (Skill 1.1)

   A. there is a one-to-one correspondence between letters and sounds.

   B. phonemes are the smallest unit of sound.

   C. consonants are phonemes.

   D. alliterative words result in different meanings.

   Answer: A. there is a one-to-one correspondence between letters and sounds
   Options B, C, and D are all true statements about phonemes, but they do not apply to phonetic languages. Only Option A is true of a phonetic language; that is, in phonetic languages, there is a one-to-one correspondence between letters and sounds. With 26 letters and 44 sounds, English does not qualify as a phonetic language.

   DIRECTIONS: Use the information below to answer the questions that follow.

   Ms. Ailara's seventh-grade ELLs are assigned a partner and each pair of students has a script of dialogue that they will follow. Below is part of an example of one of the scripts.

   Student 1: *Hello. My name is _____.*
   What is your name?

   Student 2: *Hello. My name is _____.*
   How are you today?

   Student 1: *I am fine. How are you?*

   Student 2: *I am fine. Thank you. What have you been doing?*

   After discussing the experience with her students, Ms. Ailara shows a short video where two students meet and greet each other at a party in a more informal manner, using slang and abbreviated word forms. The class discusses the difference between what they have seen and what they experienced in their earlier activity.

2. **By using scripted dialogue, the teacher demonstrates that she knows the importance of which of the following?**
   (Rigorous) (Skill 1.1)

   A. Having two students speak together–one experienced in English while the other is not

   B. Teaching students how to speak in complete sentences

   C. Using set dialogues to help students learn the patterns of English discourse

   D. Developing students' comfort level with each other

   Answer: C. Using set dialogues to help students learn the patterns of English discourse
   The best option is C because practicing in pairs and using a set

question-and-answer format helps both students learn the structure of discourse and how to process information. Option A is not correct as there is no indication that one student is more proficient in English than the other. Option B is incorrect as there is no indication that teaching is taking place. Option D is not correct because the script indicates that students are learning patterns of accepted English greetings.

3. **The video of the students greeting each other at a party is an example of which type of language usage?** *(Average) (Skill 1.2)*

   A. Standard American English usage

   B. Formal language register

   C. Academic discourse

   D. Social register

Answer: D. Social register
The use of slang and abbreviated word forms are examples of the social register used in informal conversations. These examples are also dependent on age, gender, education, socioeconomic status, and personality. Standard American English usage is the basis for regional and social registers. Formal language is not being used in the video. Academic discourse refers to formal academic learning, which is not taking place in the video.

4. **Based on Ms. Ailara's activity with her students and the viewed video, it is obvious that Ms. Ailara realizes that the affective, linguistic, and cognitive needs of ESL students should be experienced in what way?** *(Rigorous) (Skill 9.2)*

   A. Through guided discussions and open-ended questions

   B. Studied in context with examples of real-world applications

   C. Within age-appropriate academic scenarios

   D. Through carefully planned curriculum expectations

Answer: B. Studied in context with examples of real-world applications
Both activities are experiences within the context of language acquisition based on real-world needs. The use of authentic language discourse provides ESL students with opportunities to expand upon their social language development. The other options are incorrect as these are activities, not guided discussions, they are social, not academic, scenarios, and there is no indication of curriculum expectations given.

5. **Which one of the following is an example of code switching?** *(Average) (Skill 1.2)*

    A. Making gestures

    B. Calling a school "la escuela" when speaking English

    C. Using jargon, for example, "apps"

    D. Simplifying language for ELLs

    Answer: B. Calling a school "la escuela" when speaking English
    Switching from L2 to L1 in certain situations is called code switching. Gestures would properly be studied under pragmatics. Using modern jargon, "apps" for *applications* is simplifying language for those who know the modern technology used on phones. Simplifying language for ELLs is just that, trying to make the new language comprehensible to language learners.

6. **Which of the following researchers emphasized the importance of focusing on all four communicative language skills at the same time?** *(Average) (Skill 1.3)*

    A. Genesee

    B. Nunan

    C. Cummins

    D. Krashen

    Answer: A. Genesee
    Genesee emphasized the importance of integrated language skills. Nunan focused on authentic tasks and action research. Cummins distinguished between BICS and CALPS. Krashen theorized on the development of second-language acquisition.

7. **A high school ESL teacher introduces the following words and phrases before having a class discussion on their writing assignment for the day: "help," "don't do that," "no," "please help." These expressions represent which part of speech?** *(Easy) (Skill 1.4)*

    A. Conjunction

    B. Preposition

    C. Verb

    D. Interjection

    Answer: D. Interjection
    The words and phrases that are introduced are interjections, or exclamations, which are words that show strong feelings or surprise. Interjections are always followed by an exclamation mark. Conjunctions join together words, phrases, clauses, and sentences. Prepositions show a relationship between a noun, or pronoun, with another word in the sentence. They may also describe place, location, or time. Verbs convey an action or state of being.

8. **Which one of the following is the single most important factor affecting language acquisition?** *(Rigorous) (Skill 2.1)*

   A. Onset of puberty

   B. Baby-talk (proto-conversations)

   C. Self-confidence

   D. Comprehensible input

Answer: A. Onset of puberty
Options B, C, and D are all factors affecting language acquisition. However, the single most important factor is the onset of puberty, when a language learner begins to use a different area of the brain to learn a second language. This learner will probably find it more difficult to learn a new language than a prepubescent child. The best option is A.

DIRECTIONS: Use the information below to answer the questions that follow.

Ms. Mendoza's kindergarten ESL class is a busy place. A classroom observer notes that Ms. Mendoza's students are paired up or work in groups in a problem-solving, discovery format to learn basic numerical concepts. Students are on task in the centers, speaking in both their native language and in English as they interact, often intermingling both languages into sentences. In reviewing Ms. Mendoza's student data, it is obvious that there has been a continual improvement in students' mathematical understanding.

9. **It is clear from the description of the students' behavior that Ms. Mendoza:** *(Rigorous) (Skill 2.2)*

   A. knows how to implement the district's requirement for developing cognitive growth.

   B. uses theories and research to provide the appropriate strategies for language and concept acquisition.

   C. knows how to meet the needs of individual ELLs.

   D. knows how to create a classroom structure for input and output of information.

Answer: B. uses theories and research to provide the appropriate strategies for language and concept acquisition
Ms. Mendoza's classroom is evidence of applying the findings in Collier's (1995) research, which indicates that classes in schools that are highly interactive and emphasize problem solving and discovery are likely to provide the culture necessary for natural language acquisition along with concept attainment. Option A is not correct as there is no indication that there are district requirements in force. Option C is incorrect as these activities are for all students, including ELLs, and there is no indication of differentiation in teaching taking place. Option D is incorrect as an input and output of information would require more teacher direction with follow-through from students.

10. Ms. Mendoza allows students to intermingle both languages while working in centers because she realizes that:
(Rigorous) (Skill 2.4)

A. language is acquired lineally and not influenced by individual factors.

B. students need structured activities that allow them to follow their own interests in their own time frame in a supportive environment.

C. interlanguage is a strategy used by second-language learners to compensate for lack of proficiency in the new language.

D. students need to cooperate with others, interacting and working with a native speaker of the language being learned.

Answer: C. interlanguage is a strategy used by second-language learners to compensate for lack of proficiency in the new language
Interlanguage is a stage of development for learners as they transition between their first language to the second language and is indicative of their experience with the second language. Option A is not correct as language is not acquired lineally but is influenced by individual factors. Option B is incorrect as the structure of the centers is not set up to allow students to follow their own interests. Option D is not correct because while students need to cooperate with others, the focus of the scenario is on language acquisition and usage.

DIRECTIONS: Use the information below to answer the questions that follow.

During a classroom conversation in a high school self-contained English class the following was overheard by the lead ELL teacher for the school.

Instructor: *Now who can tell me about the character's actions in the second chapter? Olette?*

Olette: *She is embarrassed.*

Instructor: *No, I want to know about the character's actions in the second chapter. Olette, can you try again?*

Olette: [struggling and not looking the instructor in the eye] *She act embarrassed.*

Instructor: *No, you still aren't telling me about the character's actions. Try again, Olette.*

Olette refuses to answer and scoots down in her seat and pretends to study the text. The instructor moves on to other students.

11. Based on the scenario, it is obvious that the instructor does not understand or is not aware of which of the following strategies?
(Average) (Skill 2.3)

A. Cognitive

B. Metacognitive

C. Social

D. Socioaffective

Answer: D. Socioaffective
Socioaffective strategies are those that help learners control how they feel while learning a second language. Options A and B are incorrect because cognitive strategies deal with the manipulation of language, and metacognitive strategies help learners become aware of their learning, and how they are learning. Option C is not correct as the situation did not take place in a social setting.

12. **The lead ELL teacher meets with the instructor and they discuss the various strategies that could have been used to bolster Olette's affective learning level. Which of the following would have been the best strategies the instructor could have used in this situation?** *(Rigorous) (Skill 2.3)*

    A. Positive acknowledgment; clarifying expectations for the answer

    B. Giving the correct answer to the question

    C. Asking another student to answer for Olette and explain why the answer was correct

    D. Repeat the question slowly and with correct enunciation of each word

Answer: A. Positive acknowledgment; clarifying expectations for the answer
With positive acknowledgment and clarified expectations for the answer

to the question, the ELL feels appreciated for her effort, making it likely that the teacher will have helped to lower her affective hindrances. Option B is not correct as giving the answer does not support Olette's metacognitive development. Option C would only cause Olette to become more reticent in answering questions. The accommodations described in Option D are unnecessary.

13. **Which one of the following is a metacognitive strategy for ELLs?** *(Rigorous) (Skill 2.3)*

    A. Setting reasonable goals

    B. Constant repetition

    C. Concentration on sounds

    D. Risk taking

Answer: A. Setting reasonable goals
Setting reasonable goals for long-term and short-term learning is a metacognitive strategy in which the learner tries to improve on his/her own learning strategies. Options B and C are part of the cognitive strategy of practicing. Option D is a socioaffective strategy.

14. Which of the following is the correct explanation of the PPP model?
(Easy) (Skill 2.5)

A. Practice, Production, and Proficiency

B. Practice, Presentation, and Production

C. Presentation, Practice, and Production

D. Production, Practice, and Presentation

Answer: C. Presentation, Practice, and Production
The correct order of PPP is Presentation, Practice, and Production, a model in which teachers present small amounts of language, give the ELLs the opportunity to practice the items, and later integrate the items into the other language in order to acquire communication (production). Proficiency is not a component of this model, but it may be a result.

15. Which one of the following statements is NOT true about instructional design?
(Average) (Skill 3.1)

A. ELLs need many opportunities to work with different people during collaborative activities.

B. ELLs' interest is maintained by combining students' interests and curriculum objectives.

C. The classroom atmosphere should be supportive.

D. Learning activities are organized to repeat the same instructional point until it is mastered.

Answer: D. Learning activities are organized to repeat the same instructional point until it is mastered
Options A, B, and C are examples of appropriate instruction to address TEKS in the language classroom. Option D is the best choice because it would be a disservice to ELLs and probably lead to boredom with language instruction.

DIRECTIONS: Use the information below to answer the questions that follow.

Ms. Nguyen, a second grade teacher, has developed a word-study activity for her class of English-speaking students and ELLs. The activity is a review from the week's lessons on complete, simple sentences. In this activity, students work with a partner to create complete, simple sentences using preselected sight words from the Dolch word list. After a brief review and modeling what constitutes a simple sentence, Ms. Nguyen gives each pair of students a set of word cards as follows:

Ms. Nguyen also gives them the following directions:

1. Working with your partner, make a sentence using these words.
2. Use as many words as possible.
3. You may not add other words.
4. Write the sentence in your journals.

16. **While observing her students, Ms. Nguyen realizes that another step added to the instructions would better support the learning of the ELLs in this activity. Which of the following would be the best addition to support the ELLs?** *(Average) (Skill 3.2)*

A. The first word needs to be capitalized, and the sentence should end with a period.

B. Read the sentence aloud to your partner. Does it make sense?

C. You may add other words to your sentence.

D. You must use all the words.

Answer: B. Read the sentence aloud to your partner. Does it make sense?
The goal of the activity is to have students create simple sentences using only the given words. By reading their sentence aloud and questioning whether it makes sense, students will make connections between what they read and what they hear, thus strengthening their knowledge of correct syntax and making connections between hearing and writing. Option A is not correct because punctuation practice is not an activity goal. Option C is not correct as students have already been instructed not to use other words, only those given. Option D is not correct because using all the given words will not create a simple sentence.

17. **On reviewing anecdotal records and finished products during this activity, Ms. Nguyen found that many of her beginning and intermediate ELLs struggled with the activity while her advanced ELL and English-speaking students were successful. Which of the following should best be considered by Ms. Nguyen for future activities?**
(Rigorous) (Skills 4.2, 4.6)

A. The difficulty level of sight words used for sentence-building activities

B. The importance of reviewing the basic structure of academic expectations, as in this case, a complete, simple sentence

C. The inclusion of native-language materials during an activity

D. The academic strengths of each student when assigning partners

Answer: D. The academic strengths of each student when assigning partners
Knowing the differences in individual academic strengths is necessary when assigning partners for an activity. The ELL teacher needs to select student partners that will provide support and strategies for their ELL counterparts. Option A is not correct because the sight words are on the pre-primer and primer levels of words on the Dolch sight word list and the nouns are from the Dolch high-frequency list of nouns—all of which are suitable for this grade level. Option B is incorrect because before students began the activity Ms. Nguyen modeled a complete, simple sentence. Option C is not correct as providing materials in a student's native language will not support the learning of the student's partner.

18. **To accommodate beginning ELLs in the class, the most appropriate strategy Ms. Nguyen should implement for this activity is to:**
(Rigorous) (Skill 6.2)

A. include sight words that are more challenging.

B. model and preteach the activity before beginning it.

C. include illustrations on the appropriate word cards.

D. allow those students to observe and not participate if they choose not to.

Answer: C. include illustrations on the appropriate word cards
Having visuals will enable beginning ELLs to successfully put the words in order to form a complete sentence. Option A is not correct as increasing the difficulty level of the sight words will not help beginning ELLs make connections to the words. Option B was already done as explained in the scenario. Option D is incorrect because the activity could easily be modified to accommodate beginning ELLs in learning how to form simple sentences in the present tense.

DIRECTIONS: Use the information below to answer the questions that follow.

Mr. Roma is presenting a new unit on insects to his fifth grade ESL science class. Based on previous lessons, he knows that his class has little knowledge of the natural world. A small portion of the discussion is given below.

Mr. Roma: *Insects are not mammals, nor birds. Rather, insects are a unique species of which there are more than 800,000 types. Some insects you may know are ladybugs, grasshoppers, beetles, and ants. There are many identifying characteristics of insects. All insects have three pairs of legs and three body parts. Now that I've given you this overview, I want each of you to read pages 45 through 69 in your science book in your groups. Are there any questions? Yes, Emmanuel?*

Emmanuel: *Um, Mr. Roma. I do not understand what insects are?*

Mr. Roma: *Insects. [He writes the word on the board.] There are more than 800,000 types of insects, or what you might call bugs. There are ladybugs, grasshoppers, beetles, and ants. [He writes the words on the board.] But there are so many more insects! All insects have certain characteristics, or*

ways, to identify them. Insects have three body parts. All insects have six legs, which are three pairs of legs. We have one pair of legs, and an insect has 3 pairs of legs. Having 3 body parts and 3 pairs of legs is a characteristic of insects. [He writes this information on the board.]

19. **Mr. Roma understands the support that is needed for his ESL students during classroom presentations and discussions. Based on this portion of the presentation it is obvious that Mr. Roma realizes the importance of: (Rigorous) (Skill 4.2)**

A. carefully listening to his students and their questions.

B. summarizing the information that he gives to his students.

C. paraphrasing the information that he presents to his students.

D. turn-taking during the conversation as he presents information.

Answer: C. paraphrasing the information that he presents to his students
It is obvious that Mr. Roma is paraphrasing the information. He is restating the information in more simplistic sentences while maintaining vocabulary and important facts. Option A is not the prime objective in this scenario. In Option B, summarizing information means to present a condensed

version of the original statement, which Mr. Roma did not do. Option D includes a discussion between instructor and student, or student to student, with set roles of speaker and listener.

20. **Based on this scenario, what is an additional resource that Mr. Roma should have provided to help his students make connections to what he was saying?**
(Rigorous) (Skill 3.2)

   A. Brainstorming opportunities to generate ideas as to what an insect is

   B. A list of vocabulary words that would be used during the lesson

   C. A copy of his discussion and notes

   D. Visual supports, such as photos, charts, and diagrams

   Answer: D. Visual supports, such as photos, charts, and diagrams
   The best option is D because visual supports will help clarify concepts and vocabulary terms as they are being used. By using photos, charts, and diagrams, those who learn best visually will begin to develop independent learning skills. Option A is not correct because Mr. Roma is providing information that he knew his students did not know. During brainstorming students contribute ideas related to the concept. Options B and C are incorrect because a list of Mr. Roma's words or notes would not have helped students during the discussion.

21. **Mr. Roma wants to support his students in learning the information about insects so they can compare insects to spiders during the next day's lesson. Which of the following would NOT help his students understand and organize information so that comparisons could be made between insects and spiders?**
(Rigorous) (Skill 3.2)

   A. After the presentation and reading the selection in groups, students web out the information learned.

   B. In groups, students will create concept maps about the subject being studied.

   C. A variety of scaffolded texts on the subject is provided to help students identify facts and details.

   D. Each student uses numerous texts on spiders and insects.

   Answer: D. Each student uses numerous texts on spiders and insects
   Students need to acquire and understand the information on the first subject, insects. In order to make a successful comparison and understanding of the information, students need to associate words or phrases with the concept. Doing two subjects at a time would be too much information. Options A, B, and C are strategies that would benefit students in this scenario.

22. Mr. Roma decides to have his students create semantic maps of the vocabulary that they are learning during this study. Which of the following skills will his ELLs develop by doing that?
(Rigorous) (Skill 6.2)

A. The ability to organize and categorize information gathered

B. The ability to make comparisons and recognize similarities between two items

C. Prioritization of the information that is gathered during the activity

D. Recognition of the sequence of the information gathered

Answer: A. The ability to organize and categorize information gathered
Option A is the correct answer because semantic mapping helps students understand vocabulary and how words are organized and connected within a given subject. Semantic mapping is not used in any of the other options.

23. Which one of the following is a scaffolding technique?
(Easy) (Skill 3.3)

A. A pretest

B. Individual projects

C. Playing games

D. Using rubrics

Answer: D. Using rubrics
Using rubrics to guide the task and illustrate the expected results is the best option. Options A, B, and C are not scaffolding techniques. A pretest is used to determine students' level of knowledge, and to plan classroom activities around this knowledge. Individual projects are poor ESOL techniques in general, especially at the lower language levels. Games could be used to reinforce language points or to lower ELLs' anxiety in the classroom.

24. In order for an ELL to fully benefit from using the Internet on a topic or concept, which of the following should be observed?
(Easy) (Skill 3.4)

A. Topics should have specific goals and be timely

B. Teachers must be computer specialists

C. Communication is not required between teacher and student

D. Results do not have to be shared

Answer: A. Topics should have specific goals and be timely
Technology is progressing rapidly, but it cannot replace the teacher or good instructional practices. Options C and D would be poor instructional practices, even without using a computer. Option B is false; teachers need not be specialists in computer science.

25. Which one of the following is NOT an effective classroom management technique?
(Average) (Skill 3.5)

A. Implementing techniques that focus on the positive

B. Anticipating possible problems

C. Teaching the expected behaviors early in the school year

D. Deciding on inappropriate behaviors as they occur

Answer: D. Deciding on inappropriate behaviors as they occur
Options A, B, and C are all effective classroom management techniques. Option D suggests a laissez-faire approach in which teachers make up the rules as they goes along. This is never a good idea. Even though unexpected events occur, it is important to have the groundwork laid for them by establishing good management techniques early on. Option D is the least effective technique and the appropriate answer.

26. Ms. Chan has made an anchor chart for her ELL middle school language arts class. The chart contains a variety of sentence stems for students to use when responding to questions in the text they are reading. For example, ____ *is similar to ___ because both are* ____. After reviewing the sentence stems with students, Ms. Chan's class is more participatory during the class discussion. Ms. Chan's activity is promoting which of the following?

(Rigorous) (Skill 4.1)

A. Listening to the information being given

B. Encouraging oral responses

C. Providing support in writing responses

D. Improving the students' reading abilities

Answer: B. Encouraging oral responses
The sentence stems provide support in students' responses to questions during class discussions. This activity is an appropriate instructional method to help ELLs' development of speaking English. Options A, C, and D are not correct as the strategy is being used during a discussion, not listening to a presentation, writing a response, or reading a text.

27. Which one of the following techniques shows how questioning should NOT be used when teaching interpersonal communication skills?
(Average) (Skill 4.2)

A. Encouraging dialogue

B. Checking for comprehension

C. Requiring a one- or two-word answer in initial stages

D. Interrogating

Answer: D. Interrogating
Options A, B, and C are all effective questioning techniques. Option D is not. When students feel interrogated or threatened by questions, they may shut down and refuse to engage in communication.

28. Which one of the following is a valid ELL instructional method for communicating with students?
(Easy) (Skill 4.3)

A. Rapid-fire commands

B. Gestures

C. Speaking normally

D. Introducing new vocabulary in sentences

Answer: B. Gestures
Options A and C are counterproductive; ELL instructors should slow the pace of their speech. Option D is probably not as effective as introducing the new vocabulary by illustrating it or building on prior knowledge.

29. Ms. Misra's ESL seventh grade biology class has been studying a variety of mammals and their body systems. During the course of their studies, students created concept maps of vocabulary and illustrations of key points for individual presentations. Before presenting their information to the class, Ms. Misra has students pair up and share their information with each other. What is the purpose of this interaction?
(Rigorous) (Skill 4.4)

A. To check for correctness of information

B. To prepare for a class assessment

C. Oral rehearsal of learning

D. Management of content information

Answer: C. Oral rehearsal of learning
This particular interaction is an opportunity for ELLs to talk with each other and share what they have learned, comparing information while developing students' oral language proficiency. Option A is not correct as Ms. Misra is having students share what they have already learned. Option B is incorrect as there is no mention of this being a pre-assessment activity. Option D is not correct as the content is already managed through the use of illustrations and content maps.

30. Which of the following differences in the English language would cause difficulties for a speaker of French?
(Rigorous) (Skill 4.5)

A.   The alphabetic writing system

B.   Multiple vowel sounds represented in spelling

C.   Rhetorical questions

D.   Reading from left to right

Answer: B. Multiple vowel sounds represented in spelling
Options A, C, and D would probably cause fewer difficulties for a French speaker since these are similar in both languages. However, the multiple vowel sounds represented in English spelling are different from French, a phonetic language with consistent grapheme-phonemes.

31. Which of the following options is a nonintrusive way to give corrective feedback on written work?
(Average) (Skill 4.7)

A.   Writing an evaluative comment

B.   Commenting on how to improve the assignment

C.   Asking the ELL to redo the assignment

D.   Thumbs up

Answer: B. Commenting on how to improve the assignment
The best option is B. An evaluative comment is an assessment, not corrective feedback. Asking an ELL

to correct an assignment without providing guidance is a wasted effort, both for the instructor and the student. A thumbs up is appropriate for an oral activity. A short comment, such as how to improve the third-person singular or prepositions, would give the ELL a starting point for improving his or her language skills.

32. Which one of the following is the least effective method of teaching vocabulary to older ELLs?
(Rigorous) (Skill 5.1)

A.   Using vocabulary words in a writing activity

B.   Activating prior knowledge

C.   Explicit strategy instruction

D.   Studying vocabulary lists

Answer: D. Studying vocabulary lists
Decontextualizing vocabulary words by studying vocabulary lists is of little help to older learners. Option A gives students an opportunity to explain their understanding of the new word or concept. Option B allows students to build on their previous experiences and language. Option C helps students understand the strategies needed to decipher new vocabulary when encountered in text.

33. **For the ELL to achieve fluency in both speaking and reading, the least effective activity for ELLs is probably:**
(Easy) (Skill 5.2)

A. ample speaking activities.

B. playing computer games.

C. reading widely.

D. singing songs.

Answer: B. playing computer games
Options A, C, and D are all effective methods of developing fluency. The speaking activities interact with the reading activities. However, in playing computer games, the player is probably not developing these skills.

34. **While analyzing the reading assessment scores of her third grade ELLs, Ms. San Miguel noticed that the ELLs' fluency scores were low. Knowing the importance of fluency, which of the following strategies would benefit her students' fluency development?**
(Rigorous) (Skill 5.3)

A. Modeled and repeated reading of familiar texts

B. Guided discussions through open-ended questions about the text

C. Skimming and scanning for specific information before reading

D. Restating information just read

Answer: A. Modeled and repeated reading of familiar texts
The modeling and repeated reading of familiar texts gives ELLs opportunities to increase their reading rates and fluency through practice. Options B and D are strategies best used to help students with comprehension. Option C is best used to help advanced readers locate and find information in a text, based on a specific question.

35. **Which of the following terms explains "it" in the sentence, "Although the aircraft had been damaged, <u>it</u> could still fly"?**
(Rigorous) (Skill 5.4)

A. Chunking

B. Anaphoric reference

C. Cohesive device

D. Idiomatic expression

Answer: B. Anaphoric reference
An anaphoric device, such as using a pronoun to avoid repetition of a noun is employed in this sentence. Chunking is understanding groups of words when reading without having to read each word individually. Cohesive devices are those language forms that indicate semantic relationships between discourse elements and hold them together in a cohesive way. Idiomatic expressions, such as the theatrical expression for good luck—*break a leg*—are not applicable in this instance.

36. Which one of the following statements about prior knowledge is false?
(Easy) (Skill 5.5)

A. Prior knowledge helps learners to understand and to remember more.

B. Prior knowledge must be activated to improve comprehension.

C. Failure to activate prior knowledge may cause poor readers.

D. Good readers may reject an author's premise if it conflicts with prior knowledge.

Answer: C. Failure to activate prior knowledge may cause poor readers
Options A, B, and D are all true statements about prior knowledge. Option C is false. Research emphasizes the importance of activating prior knowledge at all levels of student instruction, not just ELL instruction.

37. At the beginning of a new semester, Mr. Choe wants to have students in his fifth grade ESL science class introduce themselves to their classmates. Which of the following would be the best activity for students to present to accomplish this?
(Rigorous) (Skill 5.6)

A. An oral PowerPoint presentation

B. An illustrated autobiographical poster

C. A written essay to be shared with the class

D. A show-and-tell presentation format with photos and illustrations

Answer: B. An illustrated autobiographical poster
In Option B, ELLs will be able to participate by using what English they know while also communicating other points they cannot. More importantly, they will be part of a group and not singled out. In options A, C, and D, students will be presenting alone and may well not have the English skills necessary to meet expectations.

DIRECTIONS: Use the information below to answer the questions that follow.

Mr. Steiner, a language arts high school teacher, has a class of ESL students whose English-language abilities vary from beginning to advanced. Based on family language surveys, he notes that the majority of students are not exposed to English outside of the classroom.

38. What is the best purpose for having and referring to a family language survey?
(Rigorous) (Skill 5.7)

    A. To decide what strategies to use to help students with their English acquisition

    B. To determine if it would be better to begin instruction in students' native language

    C. To recognize and act on the personal factors that can affect students' English literacy development

    D. To determine what level to begin students' instruction

Answer: C. To recognize and act on the personal factors that can affect students' English literacy development
Understanding the personal factors that affect ESL students' English literacy development will enable Mr. Steiner to select the correct strategies and levels of instruction to use. Options A and D are not correct as strategies are selected after determining individual factors that could hinder language acquisition as

are selecting the correct levels of language introduction. Option B is not correct as there could well be students of many different native languages within the class with varying levels of skills in the first language.

39. Which of the following would best strengthen Mr. Steiner's understanding of his students' current second-language acquisition?
(Average) (Skill 7.3)

    A. STAAR Spanish test results

    B. TELPAS proficiency results

    C. LPAC decisions

    D. ELPS

Answer: B. TELPAS proficiency results
All ESL students in the state of Texas are required to complete the TELPAS tests in reading, writing, listening, and speaking. Based on test results, a student will be identified as beginning, intermediate, advanced, or advanced high. Option A is not correct as not all ESL students qualify for the STAAR Spanish test and this test is administered to grades 3 through 5. Option C is incorrect because the committee's decisions do not always provide enough information that will help the educator make decisions in regards to instruction. Option D is not correct as the ELPS are English Language Proficiency Standards that instructors use when developing instruction, and these are aligned with the curriculum.

DIRECTIONS: Use the information below to answer the questions that follow.

An ESL second grade teacher is teaming up with the school's Inclusion Strategist to introduce mammals to students by using technology, print materials, videos, and live examples. While preparing for the lessons, both teachers agree to help students connect to prior knowledge; they decide to begin the unit by using a graphic organizer (a concept map). In this graphic organizer, students list the four main characteristics of mammals. Then, during presentation and discussion, students fill in the organizer, discussing names of animals that they know match the information given.

40. This lesson is effective for ELLs because it helps them to develop which of the following?
(Average) (Skill 6.1)

A. Multiple perspectives of the language

B. Confidence in note taking

C. Making connections with background knowledge

D. English language attainment

Answer: C. Making connections with background knowledge
ELLs are using their background knowledge to help understand the identifying characteristics of the main subject. This activity activates prior knowledge and strengthens the acquisition of new information.

Options A and B are incorrect as there are not multiple perspectives shown in the sample, nor is this a lesson in note taking. Option D is incorrect as this activity is geared not toward learning new language, but to making connections to prior knowledge.

41. ELLs develop which of the following skills while creating their own graphic organizer or concept map?
(Rigorous) (Skill 6.2)

A. Identifying main idea and supporting details

B. Making comparisons and recognizing similarities between items

C. Organizing and categorizing information

D. Listing information in sequential order

Answer: C. Organizing and categorizing information
Graphic organizers help students organize and connect information. Option A is incorrect as identifying the main idea is not the purpose of this activity. Option B is not correct because the purpose of using a concept map is not to compare and contrast. Option D is incorrect as this activity does not have students sequence information.

42. Which one of the following is among the reasons to develop problem-solving skills in the second language?
(Average) (Skill 6.3)

A. Enhances cognition in the first language

B. Reduces tension in the classroom

C. Increases spatial skills

D. Reduces intuition

Answer: A. Enhances cognition in the first language
According to Díaz-Rico and Weed, one of the main reasons for developing cognitive processes in the second language is that it transfers to the first language and enhances the learner's cognitive abilities in both languages.

43. Which one of the following conditions might cause a previously motivated student to lose interest in school?
(Easy) (Skill 6.4)

A. Peer or familial pressure

B. Anxiety about his or her performance

C. Ridicule from native English-speaking classmates

D. All of the above

Answer: D. All of the above
There are many pressures put on some immigrants and other ELLs who try to succeed in the ESL classroom. Many are not obvious to the teacher and may subtly undermine the efforts expended in the classroom.

44. Which one of the following tests would be appropriate to screen candidates for a position as an international airport announcer?
(Average) (Skill 7.1)

A. An achievement test

B. A diagnostic test

C. A proficiency test

D. A communicative language test

Answer: C. A proficiency test
The candidate is given a proficiency test to measure the proficiency of the applicant irrespective of any prior training or specific course of instruction. The objective is to see if the candidate can do the job. An achievement test is a measure of how well a student achieved the goals of the course. A diagnostic test would identify the strengths and weaknesses of a learner. A communicative language test emphasizes the importance of a candidate's ability to communicate.

45. Which one of the following is an example of alternative testing? *(Average) (Skill 7.2)*

A. Unit exams

B. TOEFL

C. Experiments and/or demonstrations

D. AAPPL

Answer: C. Experiments and/or demonstrations
Unit exams are examples of language achievement tests. Both TOEFL and AAPPL are examples of language proficiency tests. The correct option is C, a form of alternative testing.

46. A tenth grade ELL who enrolled during the 2013–14 school year is currently receiving special education services and is found to have a disability that severely affects his academic progress. Based on this information, his teacher approaches the ARD committee and LPAC to verify the level of STAAR test that he will take. What would be the proper test to administer to this student? *(Rigorous) (Skill 7.3)*

A. STAAR Alternate

B. STAAR L

C. STAAR Modified

D. STAAR Spanish

Answer: C. STAAR Modified
This student meets the requirement for the STAAR Modified test. STAAR Alternate is not appropriate because the student does not suffer from a significant cognitive disability. STAAR L is for students who require a linguistically accommodated version. STAAR Spanish is for students in grades 3 through 5.

47. Brittany, an ELL fifth grade student, passed the STAAR exam with commendations in reading, writing, and mathematics. She also maintained straight A averages in grades 3, 4, and 5. Based on this information, the LPAC decided to exit Brittany from the ESL program. Based on the LPAC decision, you can assume that Brittany scored which of the following on her TELPAS exam? *(Easy) (Skill 7.4)*
A. Beginning

B. Intermediate

C. Advanced

D. Advanced high

Answer: D. Advanced high
A Language Proficiency Assessment Committee (LPAC) will not consider exiting a student who scores less than advanced high. Brittany's grades and STAAR results would also be taken into consideration.

48. Which of the following assessments is used as an accurate measure of student achievement in reading, writing, mathematics, science, and social studies?
(Easy) (Skill 7.5)

A. TAKS

B. AAPPL

C. TELPAS

D. STAAR

Answer: D. STAAR
The State of Texas Assessments of Academic Readiness (STAAR) is for all students and is used as a gauge for district and school accountability. The TAKS has been replaced by STAAR. The ACTFL Assessment of Performance toward Proficiency in Languages (AAPPL) is reserved for ELLs. The Texas English Language Proficiency Assessment System (TELPAS) provides data on all ELLs' performances from one year to the next.

49. The purpose of assessment is:
(Average) (Skill 7.6)

A. diagnostic and ongoing.

B. to judge a student's learning.

C. to compare student performance against grade-level standards.

D. All of the above

Answer: A. diagnostic and ongoing
The distinctions between assessment, evaluations, and testing is fine but important. Evaluations are used to judge a student's learning, and tests compare a student's performance. Assessment is diagnostic and ongoing.

50. Which of the following legislative acts or Supreme Court rulings prohibits schools from excluding students from federal education programs?
(Rigorous) (Skill 8.1)

A. Civil Rights Act of 1964

B. *Lau* v. *Nichols*

C. *Castaneda* v. *Pickard*

D. No Child Left Behind Act

Answer: A. Civil Rights Act of 1964
Many different legal precedents have paved the way for children to receive formal education in the United States. One of the first and farthest reaching was the Civil Rights Act of 1964, which established that schools, as recipients of federal funds, cannot discriminate against ELLs.

51. Which of the following is NOT an ESL pull-out model?
(Average) (Skill 8.2)

A. Grammar-based

B. Communication-based

C. Self-contained

D. Content-based

Answer: C. Self-contained
Options A, B, and D are all English as a Second Language pull-out models. Option C is the correct answer: It is monolingual English instruction in a regular classroom.

52. Which of the following factors will have an influence on the decision of which type of ESL program is chosen for a school district?
(Average) (Skill 8.3)

A. School demographics

B. Nearby magnet school

C. Availability of resources

D. All of the above

Answer: D. All of the above
In these days of tight budgets and vocal community feelings, all of the factors listed play a part in the decision of school administrators and local authorities when choosing which school programs to implement.

DIRECTIONS: Use the information below to answer the questions that follow.

During Mr. Antoine's initial observations of his new middle school students, he overhears the following conversation between two girls.

Xochitl: *Hi! My name is Xochitl. We are sitting together in math. What's your name?*

Jasmin: *My name is Jasmin.*

Xochitl: *Are you excited about school?*

Jasmin: [shrugs] *English not good. I guess?*

Xochitl: *Want to meet my friends?*

Jasmin: *No, no. I not talk good. I need study.* [Jasmin walks away.]

Over the next several weeks, Mr. Antoine realizes that Jasmin does not interact with other students and will not participate in class discussions over topics and concepts. Knowing that this affects her oral-language development, he creates lessons and activities with instructional goals to increase Jasmin's oral-language proficiency among her peers.

53. **Which of the following strategies should Mr. Antoine use to best help Jasmin at her current level of oral-language proficiency?** *(Average) (Skill 8.4)*

A. TPR

B. Dialogue journals

C. CALLA

D. Reciprocal teaching strategy

Answer: C. CALLA
The Cognitive Academic Language Learning Approach (CALLA) prepares students to participate in content instruction, and students are taught to use learning strategies for comprehension and retention of concepts. Total Physical Response (TPR) is a joining of language and physical movement, such as gestures with commands. Dialogue journals focus on the development of writing more than oral proficiency. Reciprocal teaching focuses on the development of reading comprehension strategies.

54. To best meet the instructional goals for Jasmin, Mr. Antoine should create lessons that include:
(Rigorous) (Skill 9.5)

A. the rules of polite conversation.

B. class discussions reviewing why each lesson is important.

C. silent, sustained reading.

D. small-group work that incorporates speaking activities.

Answer: D. small-group work that incorporates speaking activities
With Option D, Jasmin will be in smaller, more supportive groups, which will encourage her to speak with her peers while also receiving support in her acquisition of language. Option A is not correct because discussing rules of conversation will not meet Jasmin's needs. Option B is not correct as a class-wide discussion does not address Jasmin's hesitancy to speak in a large group. Option C is not correct because silent, sustained reading will not help Jasmin develop oral fluency among her peers.

55. Which one of the following instructional techniques is most appropriate for children during the "silent period" of language learning?
(Average) (Skill 8.4)

A. Computer games

B. TPR

C. Lectures

D. Drills

Answer: B. TPR
Psychologist James Asher developed Total Physical Response (TPR) for developing language learners. Input and gestures are comprehensible and allow the learner to progress through a process similar to the way young children learn their first language. In this activity, ELLs are not required to talk, that is, produce language.

56. During class discussion in Ms. Baxter's eighth grade ESL American history class, Fong participated in the discussion but would not look Ms. Baxter in the face when responding to questions. In conferencing with Fong's other teachers, Ms. Baxter found that this was a common behavior in all his classes. Wanting Fong to participate more fully in class, Ms. Baxter would best take which course of action next?
(Rigorous) (Skill 9.1)

A. Speak with Fong to determine the reason for his evasive participation

B. Research Fong's cultural customs

C. Work with Fong one-on-one to develop classroom participation skills

D. Discuss with Fong expectations for participation in the academic classroom

Answer: B. Research Fong's cultural customs
Researching cultural customs will help the instructor learn how best to help the ELL with language acquisition. Option A may put Fong on the defensive, and he could well not understand the purpose of the discussion. Options C and D are incorrect because as stated, Fong already participates in class.

57. Which one of the following is NOT a characteristic of culture affecting an ELL's language learning?
(Average) (Skill 9.1)

A. Reason for immigrating to the U.S.

B. Language

C. History

D. Arts

Answer: A. Reason for immigrating to the U.S.
Options B, C, and D are all features of the culture of the ELL's background. Reasons for immigrating to the U.S. are not. They may simply be an expedient, such as refugee groups fleeing conflicted zones.

58. **Which one of the following is NOT a valid reason for studying the history and art of an ELL's culture?**
(Average) (Skill 9.1)

A. Helps students to broaden their knowledge base.

B. Encourages critical thinking.

C. Leads to greater understanding among people.

D. Disputes claims of superiority of the native culture.

Answer: D. Disputes claims of superiority of the native culture
A classroom activity is being used to demonstrate dominance of one culture at the expense of the other. This tactic encourages prejudices and is at odds with modern ESOL practices and theories. The goals of options A, B, and C are to tap into the interests and talents of ELLs as well as encourage greater understanding among all students in the class, school, and community.

59. **Which one of the following approaches ignores most Native American cultural beliefs?**
(Rigorous) (Skill 9.1)

A. Allow students to work as a team.

B. Utilize learning in natural settings.

C. Encourage the competitive spirit of the individual.

D. Recognize the importance of silence.

Answer: C. Encourage the competitive spirit of the individual
It is important that instructors know the cultures within which they are working. In general, Native Americans work well as teams, like learning in natural settings, and may use silence as a power tool. Rarely do they like to compete as individuals.

60. **Which one of the following is NOT a task-based activity?**
(Average) (Skill 9.2)

A. Numbering a group of items in the correct order

B. Labeling a map with the correct words

C. Role plays

D. Memorizing a list of spelling words

Answer: D. Memorizing a list of spelling words
Option D, rote memorization, is not a task-based activity. The other options are task-based activities in that they might require members of a group to achieve an objective and express it in such forms as rearrangement of jumbled items, a picture, or an oral activity.

61. Which one of the following would probably lead to language-minority parents participating in their children's education? *(Average) (Skill 9.3)*

A. Flyers sent home inviting parents to the school

B. Cultural activities explaining U.S. holidays, for example, Thanksgiving

C. Instructional materials for parents to use to support learning

D. Administrators trained to service language minority groups

Answer: D. Administrators trained to service language minority groups
Options A, B, and C give little support to parents who are probably struggling with their own language learning, especially if the materials are in English. The correct answer is D, in which administrators are trained to support parents and the community with services designed for minority groups—specifically, those parents who are learning English, about the U.S. culture, and about support services for minorities.

62. Which of the following instructional techniques do NOT demonstrate cultural sensitivity? *(Average) (Skill 9.4)*

A. Using reading material of high literary quality

B. Keeping a teaching log

C. Using a wide variety of reading materials

D. Urging slow-responding students to speak up

Answer: D. Urging slow-responding students to speak up
Options A, B, and C demonstrate cultural sensitivity. By using reading material of high literary quality and a wide variety of it, the teacher is showing cultural sensitivity. Another method of showing this is to keep a teaching log in which the teacher notes activities and topics that make ELLs uncomfortable. Option D does not show cultural sensitivity. Some students may be slow to respond because they may need more time to formulate their answers. In many cultures, wait time for responses is longer than in English.

63. Which one of the following should be avoided when selecting reading materials for the classroom? *(Easy) (Skill 9.4)*

A. Multicultured protagonists

B. Distorted gender roles

C. Settings in different countries

D. Different genres

Answer: B. Distorted gender roles
Options A, C, and D would represent literature that would appeal to a wide variety of readers. Gender roles, elders, and families should be portrayed accurately to avoid confusing the reader.

64. Which of the following statements about culture and its manifestations is the most likely to cause learning difficulties for the ELL?
(Average) (Skills 9.4, 9.5)

A. Learning a language involves learning about the culture.

B. ELLs may not understand culture and its differences.

C. Teachers may offend students when they ignore cultural differences.

D. ELLs often believe their culture is superior to the one they are learning.

Answer: C. Teachers may offend students when they ignore cultural differences.
Teachers might unwittingly cause barriers to language learning by offending their students without knowing that they have done so. Therefore, all ESL teachers need to learn as much as they can about the ELL's culture, if for no other reason than to demonstrate respect for their students' cultures.

65. Which of the following activities is a valid advocacy for the ELL instructor to engage in?
(Average) (Skill 10.1)

A. Emphasizing culturally sensitive assessment

B. Eliminating reading programs dealing with stereotypes

C. Insisting on high quality language arts programs for young children

D. All of the above

Answer: D. All of the above
There are many ways for ELL instructors to advocate for their students. The work of the advocate is never done.

66. **The lead ESL teacher at a local elementary school has been asked to present a district workshop for new hires on the comprehension needs of primary ELLs. Which of the following would be the best types of information for the ESL teacher to provide that meet the needs of a new primary ELL?** *(Average) (Skill 10.1)*

A. How to introduce students to correct pronunciation of basic English sight words followed by memorization techniques

B. A list of cultural taboos of the various nationalities that make up the district's ELL population

C. How best to check for comprehension in the ELL and the awareness and control of using certain parts of speech

D. A detailed analysis of the various nationalities, their native language structures, and how best to implement the ELPS

Answer: C. How best to check for comprehension in the ELL and the awareness and control of using certain parts of speech
Option C is the best choice as the teacher's first goal should be to help ELLs with comprehension, or understanding the language, and to be aware of the certain parts of speech that can be confusing, such as homophones, idioms, and so on. Option A is incorrect as neither of these types of strategies would be beneficial for helping primary ELLs with comprehension. Options B and D are not correct as neither of these will not support the workshop's goal.

67. **Which of the following is a way to include all the community stakeholders in school activities?** *(Easy) (Skill 10.2)*

A. Parent-teacher organizations

B. Tutors

C. Room parents

D. All of the above

Answer D. All of the above
By using all the resources available to the school, the school should have strong community support if problems occur.

68. **The lead ESL teacher in a middle school's language arts program holds a monthly meeting with her ELLs' families to provide information and encourage participation in classroom projects. This practice shows that the teacher is aware of which of the following factors that affect language development?** *(Rigorous) (Skill 10.2)*

A. Family involvement provides students with opportunities for academic communication.

B. Families with positive experiences of school and learning are more likely to have children who develop English-language proficiency.

C. The more information family members have about language instruction, the better able they are to teach their child the intricacies of the language.

D. Through these meetings, ELLs' family members are better able to determine the effectiveness of the ESL program.

Answer: B. Families with positive experiences of school and learning are more likely to have children who develop English-language proficiency
The best option is B because ELLs and family members who have positive experiences with education are more likely to receive the support needed to be successful in learning. Option A is not correct because family members might not have the academic language necessary for effective communication. Option C is not correct because family members are not native English speakers and would not know the specifics of the language. Option D is incorrect because it is up to the district to select and determine a program's effectiveness.

69. **Which one of the following is a valid way to communicate data about students?** *(Easy) (Skill 10.3)*

A. Parent-teacher conferences

B. Phone calls to parents

C. Newsletters sent home

D. All of the above

Answer: D. All of the above
Parent-teacher conferences, phone conversations with parents, and class newsletters are all ways of keeping communication open. The more ways information and data can be shared with the community's stakeholders, the stronger the grasp of such data.

70. The act before the U.S. Congress that would bring legalization to thousands of alien minors is called which of the following?
(Easy) (Skill 10.4)

A. Illegal Aliens Act (IAA)

B. Alien Minorities Protection Act (AMPA)

C. Development, Relief, and Education of Alien Minors (DREAM) Act

D. Safe Harbor Act for Minor's Education (SHAME)

Answer: C. Development, Relief and Education of Alien Minors (DREAM) Act
The DREAM Act is a proposed piece of federal legislation introduced in the U.S. Congress in 2009. This legislation provides alien minors the opportunity to earn conditional permanent residency if they graduate from U.S. high schools, are of good moral character, and have been in the country continuously for five years or more prior to the bill's enactment.

CPSIA information can be obtained at www.ICGtesting.com
Printed in the USA
BVOW10s0833190314

348139BV00004B/5/P